The Inclusive Classroom

Marquita Grenot-Scheyer, Ph.D.

Kimberlee A. Jubala, M.A.

Kathryn D. Bishop, Ph.D.

Jennifer J. Coots, Ph.D.

Teacher Created Materials

Teacher Created Materials, Inc.

Table of Contents

Introduction

At a recent planning meeting a third grade teacher voiced his concern regarding how to adapt and individualize the language arts curricula for a student with disabilities who had recently been included in his class. He remembered how hesitant he was about accepting such a student when his principal approached him at the end of last year. What was inclusion? He worried that he did not know much about this growing practice. He worried about the needs of the other children, and, perhaps his greatest fear, could he successfully include the student, given his training and experiences? That is, could he effectively design and implement an appropriate curriculum for this student whose needs seemed so different from those of the other students? It was the beginning of the second month of the new school year, and while the majority of his concerns had not come true, the curriculum issue was still of concern. Mr. Jacobs valued diversity and the importance of developing a sense of community within his class, and he had seen the benefits of having a student with disabilities in his room from the very first week. While the nondisabled students had questions about Claire, they were, for the most part, kind, helpful, and genuinely concerned about her and about how and what she learned. Claire seemed to evoke a level of empathy in them and enhance the sense of community more than he had ever seen before. At least he did not have to worry about that. Now that the routine was in place, the curriculum was really starting to "spiral up," and he was worried about Claire. How was he going to help Claire learn what she needed to learn as well as help other students in his class learn what they needed to learn?

Mr. Jacobs is not alone in his concerns and questions regarding inclusion and participation of students with disabilities in general education classes and schools. This book was written to help teachers like Mr. Jacobs get answers to the questions and concerns they have about inclusion. The questions that guide the organization of this book are the questions that are often asked as schools and districts move toward implementation of inclusive educational programs.

Rationale and History of Inclusion

What is inclusion?

Inclusion is a concept familiar to many general educators. Professional journals, teacher magazines, teacher education conferences, union meetings, and the teacher lunch room are likely places where this concept is discussed and debated. As one teacher suggests, "Inclusion is a set of values and principles" (L. Eshilian, September 1995, personal communication) that are fundamental to contemporary schools. Inclusion is really about school change to improve the educational system for all students. It means changes in the curriculum, changes in how teachers teach and how students learn, as well as changes in how students with and without disability labels interact with and relate to one another. Inclusive education practices reflect the changing culture of contemporary schools with emphasis on active learning, authentic assessment practices, applied curriculum, multi-level instructional approaches, and increased attention to diverse student needs and individualization. As suggested by O'Neil (1994–1995) inclusion is much bigger than special education and, therefore, has the potential to positively impact education for all children and their teachers. The vision (and, in some

> Inclusion is really about school change to improve the educational system for all students.

1

school districts, the reality) is that schools must change so that they become caring, nurturing, and supportive educational communities where the needs of all children and teachers are truly met (Levine, Lowe, Peterson, & Tenorio, 1995; National Coalition of Advocates for Students, 1991). This vision results in a "...future of fulfilled human and community potential, security, belonging, and valued interdependence leading to meaningful contributions for all children and members of the community" (Coots, Bishop, Grenot-Scheyer, & Falvey, 1995, p. 19).

Inclusion is generally regarded as the placement of students with disabilities in neighborhood schools and general education classrooms with peers their own age. Primary placement in the general education classroom allows for membership and the development of a sense of community for all students.

A critical component necessary to the successful inclusion of students with disabilities is the provision of appropriate supports and services for the student. These supports and services include whatever is necessary for the student to be successful in the general education environment. Such supports may include (but are not limited to) materials (Braille textbook, name stamp, and talking notebook), personnel (communication specialist, instructional aide), or specialized equipment (wheelchair, adapted desk). In addition, collaboration with families, general and special educators, administrators, paraprofessionals, and related service personnel is essential to best meet the needs of both the student and his/her teachers (Falvey, Grenot-Scheyer, Coots, & Bishop, 1995).

How is inclusion different from mainstreaming or integration?

Current models of inclusive education have been influenced by past practices of mainstreaming and integration. As students with disabilities have moved progressively closer to the mainstream and their nondisabled peers, they have moved from placement in separate schools and centers, to special day classes on general education campuses and then to regular classes for some or part of the day. Integration typically means that students with disabilities attend a special day class located on a general education campus with opportunities to be mainstreamed or participate in some part of the general education day. Such participation may be limited to recess and lunch or may include time in the general education classroom to access the core curriculum. Two key differences between these models and inclusive education has to do with ownership and support. That is, who is the teacher with primary responsibility for the stu-

> Current models of inclusive education have been influenced by past practices of mainstreaming and integration.

2

dent, and what is the nature of support that is provided to that student and his/her teacher? In inclusive models, the general education teacher is the main teacher responsible for the student's education with support provided by special education staff.

Is inclusion a new concept?

Inclusion is not a new concept or a new way to deliver special education services and supports to students with disabilities. Many students with disabilities have attended general education classes throughout their school years. For the majority of students with significant disabilities, however, the opposite has been true. These students and their families have had to endure years of rejection and segregation in society and continue to be excluded from participating in schools and classrooms attended by their sisters, brothers, and neighbors without disabilities (Falvey, Grenot-Scheyer, Coots, & Bishop, 1995). The cost of such segregation has been great in terms of children with and without disabilities having limited opportunities to learn from, develop relationships with, and grow to accept each other.

> Inclusion is not a new concept or a new way to deliver special education services and supports to students with disabilities.

What is the legal basis for inclusion?

The right to attend general education classes alongside nondisabled peers has always been a placement option guaranteed by the landmark legislation, PL 94-142, the Education for All Handicapped Children Act (EAHCA) of 1975 (now reauthorized and known as IDEA: Individuals with Disabilities Education Act, 1990). A growing knowledge base about methods to successfully include students and numerous court cases have defined and refined the concept of the least restrictive environment which is fundamental to an understanding of inclusive educational practices. Since EAHCA was first passed, the least restrictive environment has been defined as:

...to the maximum extent appropriate, handicapped children, including those children in public and private institutions or other care facilities, are educated with children who are not handicapped, and that special classes, separate schooling, or other removal of handicapped children from the regular educational environment occurs only when the nature of severity of the handicap is such that education in regular classes with the use of supplementary aids and services cannot be achieved satisfactorily (Section 1412[5][B]).

While this legal right is guaranteed by federal and state law, for many families, including Claire's, the process to gain entry into general education (i.e., to achieve inclusion) has not been an easy one. Claire's mother spent many months talking with school personnel prior to Claire's kindergarten year to ensure that her first placement in regular education would be a successful one. At that time, the special educators from Claire's early childhood special education program warned her mother that general educators weren't ready for and didn't want students like Claire. In spite of this, Claire's mother persisted, convinced that school would not be the only place in her daughter's life where she was not welcomed. Claire was (and continues to be) an important member of her community and is active in local church activities. As a single mother, Claire's mom had always taken her everywhere and was not about to change. After a meeting with her local school superintendent, during which time she talked about the importance of Claire attending her neighborhood school, the process of including Claire finally began.

Who benefits from inclusion?

Inclusive education is not only good for students with disabilities but, in fact, when done well, is good for all students. There are many academic and social benefits from inclusive education for students with and without disabilities and their teachers and families. For students with disabilities, attending school with nondisabled peers results in:

> Inclusive education is not only good for students with disabilities, but in fact, when done well, is good for all students.

◆ increased communication and social interaction opportunities

◆ age-appropriate models of behaviors and skills

◆ more active participation in the life of the school community

◆ increased individualized educational goals and objectives

◆ access to the rich core curriculum

◆ the opportunity to build a network of friends and other social relationships (Meyer, 1994)

Although the research regarding benefits of inclusion for nondisabled students is limited, the available studies suggest that inclusion provides many benefits for nondisabled students. For these students there are:

◆ increases in skill acquisition (Jenkins, Jewell, O'Connor, Jenkins, & Troutner, 1994)

◆ increases in positive attitudes and comfort level regarding students with disabilities

◆ increases in self-esteem

- increases in the commitment to moral and ethical principles
- increases in opportunities for warm and caring friendships to develop
- no loss of engaged time as a result of having students with disabilities in regular classes (For a review of benefits for nondisabled students, see Staub & Peck, 1994–1995)

While parents and family members of students with disabilities affirm the positive benefits of inclusion for their sons and daughters with disabilities, they also report the benefits of inclusion for the entire family. One father reported how much easier it was for his son to attend the same school with his brothers. There was no need to transport him to a separate school or separate afterschool activities any longer. For this family, inclusion opened the door to the rest of the community through involvement in their neighborhood school. Another mother reports how inclusion resulted in her friends and neighbors welcoming her back into the community (H. Sramek, June 1995, personal communication).

Finally, benefits for teachers have also been examined. Several studies have reported that teacher attitudes and practices are transformed by inclusion. In one study, initially cautious and negative attitudes were replaced by a sense of ownership and a gradual transformation to increased interaction and teaching of the student with disabilities (Giangreco, Dennis, Cloninger, Edelman, & Shattman 1993).

Portraits of Inclusion

Who are these students who are included? In the following section four students with disabilities who are included in general education classrooms are described. The intent is to share the stories of four students with different abilities and needs and to illustrate important concepts and strategies regarding inclusion as they are reflected in the educational programs of these students and throughout this book.

Eduardo is a kindergartner and the youngest child in his family. He lives at home with his older sister and his parents. This is his first year in an inclusive classroom, having spent previous years in early childhood special education classes in his district. Most of the time, Eduardo seems excited about being in school. When he is alert and awake, he follows the movements of the other children and his teacher with his bright brown eyes. The children in his class enjoy showing off their new toys to him because he always gets so excited. Eduardo has severe cerebral palsy which results in limited inten-

In the following section four students with disabilities who are included in general education classrooms are described.

5

tional motor movements, a gastrointestinal tube to receive nutrition, and uses an electric wheelchair to move around in his environment. He has limited use of his arms and legs, vocalizes loudly to make his needs known, and uses an adapted cheek switch to move his wheelchair.

Claire is a third grader who has been in regular education classes since kindergarten. She is a pretty young girl with blue-gray eyes that seem to see everything and a blonde ponytail that always seems to be in motion. Her teachers have described her as someone whose gift is to evoke kindness and caring in her nondisabled peers, and she is considered an important member of her class and school community. In reflecting on Claire's progress in recent years, Carla, her mother, would never have predicted that her daughter would be where she is now. At birth she experienced anoxia which resulted in cerebral palsy, a seizure disorder, a moderate visual impairment, and developmental delays in how she learns and communicates.

> **Tameka is learning to ask for a break or a different activity when she feels that she might not be able to control her behaviors.**

Tameka is a fifth grader with boundless energy and a unique sense of humor. Tameka lives at home with her mother and father. Tameka has been labeled as autistic, which she describes as having a brain that works differently. After being included in general education classes for the past four years, Tameka's teachers have developed several strategies to help her access the core curriculum. Tameka grasps new material quickly when it is paired with diagrams or pictures. Math is a strength for Tameka, especially when manipulatives are used. Reading and writing remain difficult for Tameka because of a learning disability. Tameka has some unusual and disruptive behaviors which sometimes frighten both her and her classmates. Tameka is learning to ask for a break or a different activity when she feels that she might not be able to control her behaviors. She is learning to monitor her tone of voice and to choose appropriate vocabulary when she talks to her peers. Tameka loves drama, and she delights in directing her friends in mini-plays during recess.

Thang is beginning sixth grade this year, and he is both excited and scared. Thang lives at home with his mother, his maternal grandmother, and his five brothers and sisters. Thang has a kind, gentle nature and is described by his peers as being quiet and shy. Thang is a talented artist, and he almost always chooses drawing as a free-time activity. Thang's peers will often ask for help from him with drawing or other artwork. Thang has a great deal of difficulty with school. With identified learning disabilities in reading, writing, and math, Thang struggles with many traditional school assignments. Short-term memory problems also compound his difficulty in learning new content and vocabulary. Thang is currently receiving support from the speech and language specialist, and extensive assessment was conducted to determine that Thang's academic difficulties were related to a specific learning disability rather than due to his second language acquisition. Thang's teachers are impressed with the fact that Thang wants to learn and that he continues to try hard to learn new material. It seems, however, that Thang frequently will cry or become withdrawn when he is frustrated with his schoolwork. Thang's teacher is consulting with the school counselor to see if there are additional strategies to help Thang be more successful at school. More about these students in inclusive schools will be described throughout the rest of this book.

How can I provide information to others who have questions about inclusion?

Because inclusion may be a new concept at a school, there are likely to be many people who have questions. Parents of children without disabilities may worry about inclusion hampering the progress of their children. Cafeteria workers, custodians, and school secretaries may be confused by the change in how students with disabilities are educated. Administrators may be uncertain of their roles. Some strategies that may be helpful are to have open meetings on the topic of inclusion and invite panel members from other inclusive programs who share similar roles with those who are concerned. Question and answer brochures can be developed and distributed. School-wide inservices can be held, and inclusion can be a topic for a PTA focus session. Most concerns arise from a lack of information or understanding, so the more information that can be provided, the greater the acceptance and change can be. Information of a general nature on inclusion is most helpful and protects the dignity and privacy of individual students.

Information of a general nature on inclusion is most helpful and protects the dignity and privacy of individual students.

So, is inclusion a good idea?

Absolutely. This option should be easily available to all families and their children. It has been suggested that whether or not to "do inclusion" is a question guided by our values as a society. All students benefit from attending schools that "teach, model, and promote understanding and appreciation of diversity and engage in practices that result in successful inclusion of all students without exemption" (Coots, Bishop, Grenot-Scheyer, & Falvey, 1995, p. 14). Therefore, the question that should be asked and answered is "How is inclusion best done?" While we do not have all the answers, this book was written to help provide some answers to questions educators and families have been asking as they move towards more inclusive educational models. At the end of this book, you will find a list of resources that will provide additional information about inclusion and how to do it well. In the following chapters, issues surrounding support and collaboration, the Individualized Educational Plan, assessment and evaluation, curriculum, and instructional strategies are presented. A description of typical days for two students with disabilities in inclusive classrooms is also included to help the reader see the various components of inclusion.

Support and
Collaboration

Will there be support for inclusion?

An inclusive model of education requires the establishment of a collaborative ethic and shared ownership of all students. Through such a collaborative team effort, specialized supports can follow students to general education classrooms and allow all students to develop and learn. Such supports might include assistance from a specialist to adapt activities from the core curriculum to meet the individual needs of the diverse learners in the general education classroom. The specialist will need to collaborate with the general education teacher regarding key components of the core curriculum and the classroom learning environment to design adaptations that will allow the diverse learners in the class to meaningfully participate in classroom activities. By coming together and sharing expertise and support in such a manner, the needs of all students can effectively be met in general education classrooms.

An inclusive model of education requires the establishment of a collaborative ethic and shared ownership of all students.

Who helps support the child?

Support is best provided by a team of individuals who have expertise in the child's areas of need. The team would include the child, the child's general education teacher, the child's parents, various specialists, as well as peers in the classroom. However, there is sometimes a rush to provide more support than is needed. For example, a parent or a teacher may request a full-time aide prior to assessing the child's need for such intensive support. This can interfere with classroom membership and teacher ownership of the child's education. It is important that the team examine the natural supports that are available in a classroom before adding any specialized support.

What supports can be provided?

The general education teacher would provide full access to the core curriculum, a warm and supportive educational environment, and opportunities for meaningful and active participation that will allow all students to learn. The child's parent would provide insight into the child's needs as well as help with reinforcing school learning, monitoring the child's progress, and assisting with decision making regarding school efforts to educate all children. Classroom peers can help in a number of ways. They can help provide suggestions for how a student can participate in lessons and activities. They can help to provide support and can look out for the student. Various specialists will also provide support based on the child's individual needs. The school nurse would provide support related to administering medication and other medical procedures for a child with medical needs, like Eduardo. Eduardo would also receive support from a physical or occupational therapist regarding positioning and strategies to develop fine and gross motor skills. A speech and language specialist would provide support related to developing speech, language, and communication skills if the child has communication needs like Tameka, Claire, and Eduardo. These specialists are typically labeled as related service personnel. A specialist with expertise in individualized adaptations in curriculum and instruction would provide support if the child has general delays in functioning. This person is typically called the inclusion support teacher.

> **Various specialists will also provide support based on the child's individual needs.**

What is an inclusion support teacher?

Because of the collaborative nature of inclusive models of education, it is helpful to designate a key person to organize and manage the supports and adaptations for specific students with disabilities included in general education classrooms. This person is sometimes called an inclusion support teacher. The inclusion support teacher is the person who takes the lead in organizing assessments of the student's individual needs, helps to arrange the needed support from all of the student's team members, and assists with monitoring the student's progress. He or she also needs to become familiar with each general education classroom he or she works in so that the supports fit the environment and the student. The inclusion support teacher is typically a special educator who has particular expertise in the design and implementation of individualized adaptations in curriculum and instruction for students with special needs. Any number of people can take on this job. For example, sometimes the inclusion support teacher is a resource teacher and sometimes a teacher from a self-contained special education class.

Will he or she teach in the classroom with me?

The inclusion support teacher can provide multiple and varied kinds of support which might include teaching in the classroom. For example, (1) he or she may teach a lesson to the entire class so the general education teacher will have time to adapt materials for the included student, as described earlier, (2) he or she may teach a small group during reading in order to meet the needs of the student with a disability, and (3) he or she might teach in the class to model effective individualized instructional strategies for the student with a disability.

The inclusion support teacher can provide multiple and varied kinds of support which might include teaching in the classroom.

Some of the support the inclusion support teacher provides will not involve direct teaching in the classroom. For example, (1) he or she may take responsibility for facilitating communication among team members by scheduling team meetings, maintaining ongoing contact with the parent, and filling out any necessary paperwork; (2) he or she may adapt materials to allow the student to have his individual needs met while meaningfully participating in the class lessons; (3) he or she may observe in the class and assemble portfolios to assess the child's needs and present levels of performance, as well as to monitor the effectiveness of the supports being provided; (4) he or she may help to determine and/or develop appropriate individualized curricular adaptations and instructional strategies for the included student; (5) he or she may provide moral support as the general education teacher works through solving an issue that has arisen in the classroom; and (6) he or she may take the student or a group of students out of the classroom for an activity designed to meet the student's individual needs. It is recommended that such pull-out occurs only if this pattern of delivering instruction is part of the school culture, that is, if all students receive instruction in multiple and varied ways and are moving in and out of the classroom to receive such instruction. Too much pull-out or a pull-out only for specific students can be stigmatizing and can interfere with the goal of having the included student be a member of the classroom.

Does the inclusion support teacher work only with the student with disabilities?

While the inclusion support teacher will have a student or students who are identified as requiring their support, most inclusion support teachers and general education teachers report that they indirectly and directly support all students in the class. For example, one general education teacher said that the individual adaptations designed by the inclusion support teacher for the student with disabilities were very helpful in meeting a variety of individual needs, as well as gave her some good ideas regarding adaptations for other diverse learners in her class. Other general education teachers report general benefits from having another adult in their classroom, such as a feeling that they were not alone, that they had someone to be a sounding board, and had someone to turn to if they had questions. More and more schools are, in fact, providing services for all students, using an interdisciplinary team model, to share expertise and resources to provide comprehensive and effective educational and other services for all children.

Students will receive support from these specialists based upon their needs as identified on their IEP.

What about the other specialists?

As noted earlier, related service personnel includes speech and language specialists, physical and occupational therapists, adaptive physical education teachers, school nurses, and others. Students will receive support from these specialists based upon their needs as identified on their IEP.

How and when do I interact with them?

The classroom teacher would interact with the related service personnel at meetings and also while the related service personnel are providing support to the student with disabilities. For example, Claire's speech and language specialist might come in to her class during the social studies/science period. She would assist Claire to participate in the lesson while also working intensively with her on the individualized goals of increasing sentence length, using new vocabulary, and improving articulation. While in the classroom, this specialist would also be modeling appropriate intervention techniques for the classroom teacher, instructional aide, and peers. Many related service personnel report that by working in an integrated therapy model, they not only more effectively meet the needs of the student with disabilities but they also provide important learning opportunities for the nondisabled students, as well. These students can learn important basic academic and motor skills as well as develop their abilities to be helpful, responsible, and caring. Many related service personnel and general education teachers report that it can be complicated to find time to meet, because the related service personnel most often support many students and are usually in class while the general education teacher is teaching. The inclusion support teacher may serve as the liaison between the classroom teacher and related service personnel to facilitate communication and planning. Some related service personnel report that it is very helpful to keep a journal with the teacher for ongoing communication and also to talk over the telephone outside school hours.

What is the role of the parent of the student with disabilities?

Parents play a key role for the student who is included. As they know the student best, they can be an important resource regarding individual student needs as well as supports that tend to work well for the student. They can assist with planning, implementing, and monitoring the inclusive educational program as part of the Individualized Education Plan, as will be discussed later. Some parents serve an important role by volunteering at the school or in the classroom. Tameka's mother plays an important role each year in providing suggestions and strategies that have been successful in the past and by helping others understand Tameka's unique behaviors. She also volunteers in the class each week, providing enriched science activities. Parents can also help to facilitate relationship and friendship building at school by facilitating relationship and friendship building at home through involvement in community activities such as Girl Scouts and soccer. Teachers can make many efforts to increase the participation of parents. The inclusion support teacher or someone else from the school can meet with the parents in their home to get to know the student and family better. They can invite the family to volunteer in the class and at the school or to serve on School Site Councils. They can also provide the parents with meaningful opportunities to participate in decisions about what adaptations and supports will be most appropriate for each individual student.

> Parents play a key role for the student who is included.

Does a full-time aide come with the student with disabilities?

Some students with disabilities who are included in general education classrooms may have an instructional aide who is assigned to their classroom. Teachers report such help can be essential for the success of some students in inclusive educational programs. However, for many students an aide is not required and can, in fact, inhibit the success of the inclusive educational program. For example, an aide can hover near a student with disabilities and thereby prevent interactions with nondisabled peers as well as inhibit the general education teacher from taking ownership of the student with special needs. Some teachers have said they felt they relied too much on the aide to support the student with a disability in their class. This meant that the student was not a fully participating member of their classroom community. It is recommended therefore, that great care be taken in making a decision about whether or not a student requires an aide to be effectively included, as well as in determining the specific periods during the day when assistance is needed.

How do I best "use" the aide?

The aide's support can best be used to assist the teacher to arrange a positive learning environment that allows ALL students to do their personal best. He or she may teach small groups, prepare materials, monitor behavior, and generally assist the classroom teacher as needed. Part of the aide's responsibilities in arranging a positive learning environment will be to provide the direct and indirect types of support for the student with disabilities as have been described previously, such as adapting materials or checking the physical accessibility of a field trip destination.

The aide's support can best be used to assist the teacher to arrange a positive learning environment that allows ALL students to do their personal best.

Can the aide work with other students in the classroom?

Whenever possible, the aide should work with other students in the classroom. This may be the best way to help the student with disabilities develop his/her skills as has been described previously. It is definitely the best way to ensure that the aide's presence in the classroom meets the goal of enhancing the positive learning environment for ALL students.

Who supervises and trains the aide?

Because they will be the primary supports for the included student, it is best if the aide, the classroom teacher, and the inclusion support teacher function as a team. The classroom teacher and inclusion support teacher should, therefore, share the responsibility for supervising and training the aide and making sure that he or she is prepared to provide the individualized supports required by the included student. The teacher and aide team may require ongoing assistance from the specialists involved with the student with a disability to help them provide appropriate and adequate supports for the student. The more responsibilities an aide is required to fulfill, the more extensive his or her training will need to be and the more ongoing monitoring and coaching will be required. For example, the aide may be responsible for physical positioning and providing nutrition for students like Eduardo and would, therefore, need training in correct positioning and use of the gastrointestinal tube. Part of her daily duties would then be to take Eduardo to the nurse's office at the start of lunch, feed him through his gastrointestinal tube, and then return with him to the cafeteria to allow him to sit with his friends to socialize during lunch. The nurse would regularly monitor the aide while performing these duties to ensure that these supports were being provided in an appropriate manner. The aide may be responsible for facilitating appropriate communication and interaction for students like Claire. He would then need training in arranging opportunities for interaction, as well as assisting Claire to print out a hard copy of her messages from her Canon Communicator, a small communication device. The aide may be responsible for assisting with implementation of Tameka's positive behavioral support plan. She would then need training in identifying triggers for Tameka's disruptive behaviors so that she could intervene and assist Tameka to ask for a break or a different activity, as appropriate. The aide may be responsible for adapting academic materials for students like Thang. She would then need training in identifying the appropriate number and type of problems on Thang's math worksheet at the start of each math period. Depending upon individual student needs and the previous experience of the instructional assistant, ongoing support and training would also be necessary as change and growth occurred throughout the year.

General education teachers involved in inclusive educational programs report that peers can provide many supports.

How does the child provide support for his/her own inclusive program?

The child with disabilities can provide important information that can enhance the success of the classroom experience. He or she may share particular interests, favorite strategies, and fears or concerns that impact his/her ability to be an effective learner in the classroom. For example, Tameka has made it very clear that when peers are arguing about who gets to sit by her or work with her, she may need to scream. Thang has told his teachers that he works better when he does not have to sit by peers who talk a lot.

How can peers provide supports?

General education teachers involved in inclusive educational programs report that peers can provide many supports. Some peers are adept at suggesting meaningful and relevant curricular adaptations. Their teachers report they are great problem solvers. Other students are motivated by being a buddy to a student like Eduardo who requires assistance to move from the classroom to the playground or to keep his head up during the math group. Such student to student support can facilitate a sense of community, belonging, and interdependence for all students and help them to develop the skills neces-

15

sary to function in an increasingly diverse world. Fostering interdependence and the sense of a classroom as a community of learners requires that such concepts be continually reinforced through general classroom rules, classroom instructional strategies, and specific classroom activities. Examples of classroom rules that can build a sense of community and thereby support inclusion efforts include the following: "Be kind and considerate of others," "Be a good cooperator," and "Be helpful." Instructional strategies such as cooperative learning can also foster feelings of the classroom as community. These and other strategies will be described more fully in the instructional strategies chapter.

Do peers miss out on their own work by helping?

When the classroom atmosphere is one in which all students cooperate to help each other learn and do their personal best, students do not miss out on their own work by helping others. In fact, many students have their own learning reinforced by teaching others. Fast finishers are sometimes motivated by being able to help other students with their work when their own work is done. One recent study has found that nondisabled students continue to achieve and make progress on their own work when helping in cooperative groups with students with disabilities (Hunt, Staub, Alwell, & Goetz, 1994). We do caution, however, that teachers monitor the progress of students and the amount of time being spent helping others.

> In a classroom where a strong sense of community is facilitated and fostered, helping one another will become a natural process.

In a classroom where a strong sense of community is facilitated and fostered, helping one another will become a natural process. All children, with and without disabilities, should have the opportunity to be the person providing assistance as well as the one receiving assistance. There are many activities that can support this sense of teamwork. Car and Driver (on page 18) is an example of a game that emphasizes risk taking but also underscores the value of supporting one another.

How do all of these people work together?

As has been described, there are many individuals who participate in the planning and delivery of the educational program for students with disabilities who are included in general education classrooms. Such collaboration requires that people develop relationships based on a collaborative ethic and shared ownership of all students. Over time, individuals can establish credibility and gain acceptance, confidentiality, and trust, all of which are necessary for effective collaboration. Relationship building also requires acknowledgment of each other's area of expertise and active, genuine, and meaningful involvement of all team members involved in supporting the student with disabilities. Team members may need to develop collaborative skills to make sure every voice is heard. Basic social and communication skills, as well as techniques for shared decision making, conflict management, and values and role clarification can be developed through parent training, preservice teacher training programs, inservice staff development, practice, and coaching, and will assist effective collaboration efforts. Team members may also require training in facilitating effective and efficient meetings. Finally, effective collaboration requires that collaborative structures and routines be put in place. One such structure is a school site team (Thousand & Villa, 1990). This team has the responsibility to plan, implement, and monitor the educational program. This team typically consists of the key players as have been described throughout this chapter.

When does this team meet?

The amount of meeting time needed for school site teams tends to vary according to the needs of the student who is being included and according to the team members' prior experience with inclusive educational programs. Meetings can be called by any team member at any time. The most important thing to keep in mind is that the team must meet at some regular interval. In order to collaborate effectively, teachers, related service personnel, and parents must come together to talk, plan, and problem solve. Once a month or bi-monthly is the typical frequency of meeting time. The general education teacher or the inclusion support teacher typically runs these meetings. Because administrators and teachers recognize the importance of collaboration, many schools are scheduling opportunities for collaboration within the school day. For example, one school district has a minimum day every Wednesday. School hours are a little longer on the other days to allow for this time. The shortened day allows teachers and parents to have time to meet and therefore encourages collaboration on many key issues. To encourage participation by working parents, school site teams can also meet in the evening or another time that is convenient for the parents and school personnel.

Can you do inclusion alone?

Successful inclusion requires a team effort. The team can work together to plan and implement inclusive educational models and collaboratively solve problems as they arise. Such a team effort requires time as described above, but, most importantly, it requires a commitment and a belief by all members of the team that all students belong and that the learning and achievement of all students is the responsibility of each team member. It also requires a belief that the necessary supports can be brought to the classroom to help each individual student learn and succeed.

The team can work together to plan and implement inclusive educational models and collaboratively solve problems as they arise.

17

Car and Driver

Goal: To develop trust in each other; to develop concern and compassion for each other; to work for the good of the group.

Materials: None

Directions: Children choose a partner. One partner starts as the driver; the other child starts as the car. The "car" puts his/her hands in front of him/her. These are the bumpers. The car closes his/her eyes. The driver is now responsible for his/her car, and no collisions are allowed. The driver places his/her hands on the steering wheel (shoulders). The driver backs the car out of the driveway. Have the students use their imaginations to take right and left turns, maneuver around the spaces, go on ramps, over bridges, on and off the freeway, stop for red lights, etc. This should continue for about five minutes. Then, stop and ask the children how many kept their eyes shut the entire time. Ask the children how they felt when they changed places. Partners should switch so each gets the experience of being both car and driver.

Reprinted from TCM 601 Celebrating Diversity—Extended Theme, *Teacher Created Materials, 1993*

Individualized Education Plans (IEP's)

What is an IEP?

The IEP highlights the priority areas which have been identified by the team of people most directly involved with the student. The Individuals with Disabilities Education Act (IDEA) mandates that all students who have been identified as having a disability be provided with an educational program tailored to meet their individual needs. This individualized program must provide educational benefit for the child and must be evaluated in terms of meaningful progress. The development of the IEP is a collaborative process that includes collecting assessment data, identifying the student's strengths and needs, determining necessary supports and services, and delineating goals and objectives for the upcoming year. The IEP is essentially an agreement signed by teachers, parents, administrators, the student, and other participants who have helped to design a plan to address the student's unique educational needs.

> The IEP highlights the priority areas which have been identified by the team of people most directly involved with the student.

What is included in an IEP?

The IEP includes a summary of assessment information which identifies the current level of educational performance in areas specific to the individual student. For example, Eduardo's IEP may include assessment information regarding his self-help skills, motor skills, and communication skills. Tameka's assessment data may focus on information related to her academic skills and her social skills. Additional information on the assessment process is included in the next chapter.

Based on the assessment information, annual goals and short term objectives are written which identify those skills which are to be achieved within the course of the academic year. Goals and objectives for some students may focus completely on academic areas such as math, reading, and writing. Some students may also have related skill goals such as study skills, coping skills, and social interaction skills. Others students may have goals that focus on basic skills areas such as communication, mobility, self-care, and object utilization.

> The consultation model means that the therapist will provide advice and suggest specific strategies to the teacher and family that can be incorporated all through Claire's day.

Along with each goal and objective a baseline measurement is provided. The baseline provides information regarding the student's current level of performance in the specific area addressed by the objective. The objective will also include a statement of how that specific skill will be measured or evaluated by the end of the IEP period. This information aids in determining whether meaningful progress has occurred. For example, writing skills may be evaluated based upon a portfolio presentation by the student, while initiating conversations with peers might be measured by a frequency count chart developed by the teacher.

The specific supports and services needed by the student, such as physical therapy or speech therapy, will be identified in the IEP along with estimated amounts of time a student will receive services from related support personnel. How such services will be delivered is also included. For example, Claire's IEP may state that she will receive adaptive physical education for 30 minutes a week in a consultation model and occupational therapy for 45 minutes a week in a direct service model. The consultation model means that the therapist will provide advice and suggest specific strategies to the teacher and family that can be incorporated all through Claire's day. A direct service model means that the therapist will work directly with Claire, including, it is hoped, other classmates in activities that fit within the routine of the general education classroom.

IEP formats will vary from district to district, but the content remains the same. The IEP also will include a federal disability code which is necessary for funding purposes (federal and state funding may differ, based on the type of disability a student is identified as having) and relates to eligibility for special services. Though IEP formats will vary from district to district, the components remain the same.

Do all IEP goals look the same?

The goals and objectives written in an IEP are individualized, meaning that they are specific to each student and are not based on a disability label or special education program. Although several students in a classroom may share a similar disability label such as "specific learning disability," each student's IEP will have different goals and objectives based on the student's particular strengths, needs, and interests.

Because each student will have unique strengths, needs, and interests, the IEP goals identified for each student will reflect this same sense of uniqueness. Consequently, goals selected for Eduardo would likely look quite different from those identified for Thang.

Goals for Eduardo might include:

- ◆ Greet peers with eye contact and a smile.
- ◆ Choose a preferred story when presented with a selection of three.
- ◆ Drink from a cup with assistance.

Goals for Thang might include:

- ◆ Increase math computation skills using a calculator.
- ◆ Brainstorm ideas for use in paragraph writing.
- ◆ Use notes to share information in a group setting.
- ◆ Ask for help when he does not understand the directions.

What is the difference between a goal and an objective?

As the reader can see, a goal is a general statement regarding the child's need. As described earlier, the child's individualized education plan must provide educational benefit to the child and must be measured in terms of meaningful progress. To evaluate benefit and progress, the annual objectives must be capable of measurement. The measurement must be objective, documented, and related directly to the individual need, the present level of performance, and the baseline. Examples of objectives for Eduardo and Thang, based upon the stated goals are presented below.

To evaluate benefit and progress, the annual objectives must be capable of measurement.

Goal: Greet peers with eye contact and a smile.

Objective: Eduardo will greet peers with sustained eye contact and a smile when peers approach him, three of five opportunities, for a two- month period, as measured by anecdotal notes.

Goal: Increase math computation skills using a calculator.

Objective: During math time, Thang will use a calculator to check the accuracy of his computation work independently, four of five opportunities, as measured by self-evaluation and teacher checking.

How does the student's IEP relate to the core curriculum?

The IEP goals written for some students will relate directly to concepts covered in the core curriculum.

It is important to emphasize that objectives on a student's IEP can be implemented within the context of curricular activities and that they need not be considered fragmented skills which are worked on in isolation or in designated special education settings (exceptions may include certain hygiene or medical procedures). Students' success can be maximized if they are given many opportunities to practice skills in the context of interesting core curriculum activities with peers as partners and role models.

The IEP goals written for some students will relate directly to concepts covered in the core curriculum. Tameka might work on acquiring three new concepts during each unit covered in the science curriculum. Tameka might also have a goal to increase her vocabulary related to a classroom novel or a specific topic of study. During math, Claire is working on completing two and three place multiplication with carrying. For journal writing, Claire participates by telling an adult what she wants to write about in her journal.

For some students, modifications and adaptations may be developed which allow students to meet their IEP goals within activities of the core currriculum. Thang's IEP may include a goal to spell 80% of the words correctly on a weekly spelling test. It may be necessary, however, for Thang to work from a list of 10 words while other students in the classroom have an expanded list of 25 words.

For other students, tools will be specified that fit into the context of the core curriculum activities, but the student will not be expected to master the concepts being presented. For example, Eduardo may work on a goal of visual scanning during calendar time as he selects a friend to be his partner in completing this activity. This same goal could be addressed at several different times during the school day, giving Eduardo multiple opportunities to learn this skill and to meet his IEP goal.

How do I match the student's IEP with the classroom schedule?

Just as the core curriculum and the state/district frameworks serve as a roadmap for planning an educational year, the IEP serves as a roadmap for planning the educational year for a student with disabilities. The teacher then has the ability to merge the classroom map and the student's map.

Some school site teams report that a Full Inclusion Scheduling Matrix is a helpful tool to guide the merger of these maps. The Full Inclusion Scheduling Matrix can help the team in deciding what individual needs can be met throughout the scheduled activities in the general education class. It allows the parents and staff the opportunity to see how the individual student's goals are interwoven into the entire day and across the curriculum. A sample of one of these forms, filled out for Claire, can be found on page 24.

> The Full Inclusion Scheduling Matrix can help the team in deciding what individual needs can be met throughout the scheduled activities in the general education class.

Who writes, implements, and evaluates the IEP and how often does this happen?

The formal IEP document is written by a team of people, including the general education teacher, the inclusion support teacher, the parent, the student, an administrator, any related support personnel, and other student/family support people such as friends and advocates. The intent of the team is to gather the people who know the student best and who have expertise in the child's area of need so they can all share their expertise in helping to develop the plan for the year. It is an important mandate of IDEA that active parent participation be sought in the development of the IEP.

The formal IEP meeting is generally held once a year. At this meeting, the previous year's IEP will be reviewed, and plans will be made for the current year. Any team member can call an additional team meeting at any time during the year that he or she feels a change in plans is necessary.

Full Inclusion Scheduling Matrix

Student: _Clair B_

Age: _8_

Grade: _3_ General Education Teacher: _Jacobs_

Class Schedule:

Inclusion Support Teacher: _Ryan_

Date: _9/95_

School: _Miramonte_

Student's IEP Objectives	Opening	Language Arts	Recess	Math	Lunch	Science/ Social Studies	Recess	Art/ Music	Dismiss			
Math: Identify coins & values												
Follow 3rd gr. math curr.		X		X								
Quantity of work similar - same time on task		X		X		X		X				
Facilitate with at least 3 people	X	X		X		X		X				
Stay in seat	X	X			X		X					
Raise hand to request attention	X	X		X	X	X			X			
Writing: Dictate to peer or adult		X				X		X				
Check self after using restroom			X		X		X					
Speech: Improve sentence length	X	X				X		X				
P.E.: Improve motor skills			X									

Assessment and Evaluation

What is the purpose of assessment and evaluation?

The purpose of assessment is to determine a student's learning styles, strengths, needs, existing knowledge base, and gaps in knowledge. The purpose of evaluation is to determine the extent to which skills or content have been mastered after specific instruction of the material has been provided. In other words, assessment provides a teacher with information on what it is a student needs to learn and how to best teach that student; evaluation provides information on the progress the student has made or is making in any given content or skill area.

This information is helpful when determining the extent to which an IEP goal has been met or when evaluating work behaviors on a student's report card. Information regarding classroom performance along with assessment data from parents and other professionals will assist the teacher in measuring the extent to which IEP goals have been met. This same process may be used when teachers prepare for report cards and parent conferences.

The purpose of evaluation is to determine the extent to which skills or content have been mastered after specific instruction of the material has been provided.

Teachers are constantly questioning whether the information being presented in the classroom is being mastered by the students. Review of portfolios, work samples, projects, and traditional paper and pencil tests can help teachers determine the extent to which the material has been learned, as well as what modifications might be necessary. While assessment and evaluation are important requirements of the IEP process, the most important reason for collecting data on student progress is to monitor progress and make decisions regarding what to teach.

Is assessment different for students with disabilities?

For students with disabilities, assessment and evaluation take on additional purposes. Assessment is necessary for a student to be deemed eligible for special education services. The assessment instruments used and the resulting scores or information will help determine the specific disability code necessary for federal and state funding and will suggest the types of professional supports which may be most helpful. The evaluation of students with disabilities is similar to students without disabilities with the exception that the IEP dictates the specific goals and objectives which must be evaluated on an ongoing basis.

Assessment is necessary for a student to be deemed eligible for special education services.

Where do I begin?

Any sound education program must be based upon comprehensive assessment data. It is important that teachers design an appropriate assessment plan which will address the whole child. Quality assessment is based on a transdisciplinary approach in which parents and professionals work together to provide a description of the student's current performance level, strengths, interests and preferences, most effective learning styles, and the educational goals targeted for intervention.

In designing an assessment plan, the IEP team will determine the areas to be assessed, the individuals responsible for completing certain components of the assessment process, and the time line for completing the assessment. It is of particular importance that assessment be conducted by people who are familiar with the child and with whom the child feels comfortable. In addition, assessment strategies should be sensitive to the cultural and linguistic needs of the student. For example, if the Home Language survey is returned for Thang and it indicates the primary language used in the home to be Khmer, then Thang's proficiency in all areas must be assessed in his native language.

What areas will be assessed?

Most plans will consist of five areas of assessment. The areas most necessary to address for students with disabilities in the general education setting include getting to know the student as an individual, determining basic skills needs, assessing academic strengths and needs, analyzing the ability to function in classroom and school community routines, and understanding the student's learning styles.

How can I get to know the student?

Developing a relationship with a student is an essential part of being an effective teacher. To develop a relationship it is important to gain an understanding of what is important to that student and his or her family. Understanding a student's cultural background, values, and traditions, the way in which the family functions, and the expectations the student and family have of the educational system are essential steps in building a relationship. To help understand the student and to determine what will most likely motivate the student in an educational setting, knowing the student's hopes, dreams, and fears, along with those of his or her family, is essential. Knowing the likes, dislikes, interests, habits, and hobbies can provide helpful insights into who this child is on a personal level.

> Developing a relationship with a student is an essential part of being an effective teacher.

What basic skills needs will be assessed?

Understanding areas of basic skills needs such as fine and gross motor, communication, and self-care (e.g., dressing, hygiene, eating, urinary/bowel control) may be of great importance for the overall success of a particular student with disabilities. In addition, medical needs such as seizure control and monitoring, medication disbursement, and specific medical procedures (e.g., oxygen-assisted breathing, catheter care, suctioning) should be specifically addressed. The transdisciplinary role of the IEP team will ensure that a general education teacher is not necessarily responsible for assessing or perhaps even implementing such specific procedures. Rather, teacher input is necessary to determine how such needs can be accommodated in the routine of the classroom. Most basic skills needs can be met within the context of general education activities, as will be discussed in the curriculum section of this book.

How will I know about the student's academic strengths and needs?

Academic skills and needs are most often assessed through the use of formal or teacher made testing materials. Determining the level of academic skill competence and academic strengths and needs is important as it will help identify goals and objectives for each student. Students, particularly those with specific learning disabilities, may present a complex picture of strengths and needs. In order to effectively assess, evaluate, and intervene, these complexities must be sorted out. Students who struggle with reading may have difficulty in social studies or science units if content is presented and/or evaluated in a way which relies on a student's ability to read as opposed to the ability to master content-related concepts and information. If the content is presented and evaluated in ways which do not rely predominantly on reading, these students may be able to demonstrate their knowledge more successfully.

How will I assess the ability of the student to function within classroom routines?

The success of students who are included in general education classrooms often relies on how well he or she is able to adhere to the rules and regulations (stated or implied) of the school or classroom structure. The child's ability to function in classroom routines can be analyzed through systematic observation and through interviews with people who know how the child has functioned in other settings. Students who have been previously educated in special education settings may not have been required to raise their hands before responding, line up before going to lunch or recess, sit in a designated area of the classroom, ask to use the restroom or sharpen a pencil, or return materials to their proper place after use. School routines such as assembly behavior, lunchroom practices, and playground rules may have been different for students in special education environments. Students can often be mislabeled as having behavior problems when, in fact, the expectations of the setting have not been made clear or have not been fully understood by a student. Assessing the student's needs in this area can allow necessary preparation and instruction to occur which will significantly enhance the student's ability to function successfully within those contexts.

How will I assess the child's learning styles?

Whether in assessment or evaluation, a broad and comprehensive view of the student will give the teacher the best picture of the student at any given time. As many teachers know, students will demonstrate understanding of various concepts and skills in a multitude of ways. The work of Howard Gardner (1983) and Thomas Armstrong (1994) on multiple intelligences has provided a framework for understanding intelligence that requires a comprehensive analysis of a students' strengths and skills. The seven intelligences and examples of each form are provided on the following page.

> As many teachers know, students will demonstrate understanding of various concepts and skills in a multitude of ways.

- ◆ Linguistic intelligence (learns by reading, writing, and spelling)
- ◆ Logical-Mathematical intelligence (learns easily in math; learns by reasoning)
- ◆ Spatial intelligence (learns by drawing and art, reads maps and charts easily)
- ◆ Bodily-Kinesthetic intelligence (learns by doing, does well in sports)
- ◆ Musical intelligence (learns through patterning and sequencing, enjoys different kinds of music)
- ◆ Interpersonal intelligence (learns through interaction with others, socializes easily, demonstrates empathy for others)
- ◆ Intrapersonal intelligence (learns best independently, seems in her own world)

Using this model as a basis for assessment and evaluation, teachers can view students with disabilities as individuals possessing strengths in many areas of intelligence. Observing and interviewing the student and others that know him/her well can provide the teacher with specific information regarding a student's areas of intelligences and personal learning style. Such information has important curricular and instructional implications. For example, during an interview, Eduardo's mother said that he seems to love all sorts of music and musical instruments and that he appears more alert and ready to learn when music is playing. This suggests one of his areas of intelligence and his personal learning style lies in the area of musical intelligence. Eduardo's teacher has kept this personal learning style in mind as she has selected and prioritized the curriculum for him and as she plans for instruction.

> Most assessment and evaluation is ongoing, helping teachers to make appropriate curriculum and instructional decisions for each student throughout the year.

How often will I assess or evaluate the student?

It is likely that different types of assessment will be conducted at different times, by different people, and for different reasons. Assessment procedures for determining the IEP will occur on an annual basis and evaluation of the IEP goals and objectives will be an ongoing process. Most assessment and evaluation is ongoing, helping teachers to make appropriate curriculum and instructional decisions for each student throughout the year. Work samples can be collected over time in order to demonstrate improvement. The use of portfolios provides a system in which students and teachers collaboratively select evidence of growth over the year.

Anecdotal evidence regarding student performance can be collected in different subject areas using, a variety of formats. This type of record keeping is most often implemented in the context of the language arts curriculum but can easily be expanded to other academic areas. Notes can be added as teachers and students interact during conferences or as work samples are reviewed.

In addition, teachers may ask other support team members to systematically collect information regarding the strengths and needs of the student. For example, a record of the situations in which a child initiates conversation or asks for help could be kept periodically by the aide or inclusion support teacher.

How will I grade the student? Will the student get a report card?

The students progress or grades must be evaluated in terms of individual needs as identified in the IEP.

The IEP provides a context in which student progress can be evaluated. This is the legal document for which student evaluation is documented and ensures accountability of the educational process. The student's progress or grades must be evaluated in terms of individual needs as identified in the IEP.

If it is determined that in addition to the IEP, a report card will be issued, the IEP team might discuss the use of modifications to insure that this system accurately reflects a student's needs and abilities. For example, "grades" may be assigned only by effort to reflect progress rather than mastery or to indicate progress on specified IEP goals. Further, anecdotal information might be included on the report card to indicate current level of performance or to indicate the modifications currently in place. Achievement grades may also be issued but with an additional code signifying that the content was taught and mastered with the use of accommodations, adaptations, and modifications suitable to the needs of the student and is not a comparable standard of measurement for grade level work.

Managing the Curriculum

Who decides what the curriculum content will be?

Most states and districts provide teachers with curriculum frameworks based on subject areas and grade levels. In California, for example, the framework states that for social studies, all fourth grade students will study California history. Typically, it is up to the teacher to determine some of the aspects of California history that will be studied and how the material will be presented. These frameworks generally represent a culturally valued body of knowledge that all students are expected to understand and access. Access to and some understanding of this culturally valued body of knowledge is generally viewed as an important contribution to a full and valued adult life. Such access then can be considered especially important for groups at risk of being stigmatized, such as students with disabilities.

Sifting through curricular content is a task teachers continually face. Decisions on breadth versus depth of information to be presented and mastered are difficult. These choices will likely depend upon the particular group of students as well as the interests and expertise of the teacher. Determining the critical points of information for any given content area is the first step toward building a curricular unit that will benefit a heterogeneous group of students.

Sifting through curricular content is a task teachers continually face.

31

Are all students expected to learn the same thing?

Given the diversity of children in today's classrooms in terms of interests, backgrounds, and academic strengths and needs, educators may be most successful by considering curriculum content in varying levels. Determining the most critical information in each content area for students to master is an important initial step. In a heterogeneous classroom, there will likely be different objectives for different students in each content area. It may be most helpful to identify the information that most students are expected to master, given the guidelines outlined in the state or district framework. In addition, teachers will need to identify the basic concepts that are more relevant for students who have more difficulty in a given subject. Teachers will also identify additional information that students who have more advanced skills in a particular area will master. Finally, consideration is given to the content that supports a student's IEP (Individualized Education Plan) objectives and enhances his or her general knowledge base.

While the intent of inclusion is to assure that all students have access to similar curricular content, the particular content mastered by each student will vary. For example, in a lesson on plant life, all students will plant seeds, choose a light source, measure plant growth, examine plant leaves under a microscope, identify the parts of a plant, and record data. If these activities were to occur in their respective classrooms, Eduardo would be learning to control his arm movement as he scoops soil from his wheelchair tray into his planting bin. Claire would learn to count the number of seeds she is planting and copy the name of each plant in her science log. An appropriate goal for Tameka would be to ask and answer questions in group activities and to treat other people's plants and materials respectfully. Thang could work on increasing his vocabulary by drawing and labeling pictures of the plants as an alternative to the writing assignments. A recording sheet, such as the example on page 33, may be useful in helping students organize the information for their plant reports. In using this form, Eduardo might point to symbols on his communication board to be recorded by a peer. Tameka may dictate her responses while Claire or Thang might choose to draw rather than write about their experiments. Just as content to be mastered will vary from student to student, individual adaptations may be necessary to facilitate the student's ability to access the material.

> While the intent of inclusion is to assure that all students have access to similar curricular content, the particular content mastered by each student will vary.

Plant Reports

After the children have planted seeds, you may want them to report on the growth progress as it occurs. On this page you will find a number of ideas for you to use.

Sample Form

Use the sample from below as a guideline for a plant report. Copy the text onto regular copy paper or make a class-size chart and fill it with everyone's observations.

My Plant Report **Directions:** Write or draw about your plant experiment in each space.	
These are the things I used:	This is what I did:
On _____ I (day) checked my plant. This is how it looked:	On _____ I (day) checked my plant. This is how it looked:

Accordion Books

Tape several sheets of construction paper together and fold accordion-style. On each page write a different day and date along with the children's observations. You may have pairs work together on this project. They can draw pictures, write sentences, or dictate their words for you to write.

Wheels

Cut out large circles from construction paper or tagboard. Divide them into fourths. Have each child record four observations from four different days in each of the segments.

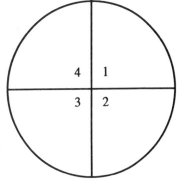

Reprinted from TCM 244 Plants—Thematic Unit, *Teacher Created Materials,* 1995

Will students who are included slow the rest of the class down in terms of content covered for the year?

Because the students will have different goals within specific content areas and classroom activities, there is no need to change the curriculum or the pace at which material is covered to accommodate a child who is fully included. By organizing the curricular content in a way that accommodates diverse needs in shared activities, teachers can ensure that students who have particular strengths in a content area are not held back by students with greater needs and that the students with greater needs are not being overlooked in order to keep moving through the curriculum.

It is essential that all students have access to all aspects of the curricular content yet be expected to master an appropriate level of the information. In the previous example, all students are expected to participate in activities designed to demonstrate plant growth and change. However, only some of the students will be expected to master the equation for photosynthesis. Students will be evaluated on the content which has been deemed most essential for them, given their backgrounds, skills, and needs.

> It is essential that all students have access to all aspects of the curricular content, yet be expected to master an appropriate level of the information.

Student's strengths and needs will vary from content area to content area. Providing all students with the opportunity to learn a shared curriculum supports the notion of the classroom as a community. Curricular content areas are part of the culture within that classroom and the different levels of content mastered are a way of celebrating the diversity within that culture. Students with disabilities are then given access to the same culture experienced by their nondisabled peers within the general education classroom. Additionally, the opportunities for experiencing a shared culture extend beyond the classroom into the school itself through lunch and recess activities, assemblies, and extracurricular activities.

How will I know if my curriculum is meaningful?

A curriculum that has meaning for students will include rich and varied experiences for all students, content that is in sync with social and cultural realities, and classroom activities that are arranged to provide a variety of learning opportunities. Meaningful curriculum allows children to both think about and learn subject matter through participation in real life learning experiences. These basic principles for developing and selecting curriculum apply to all students, including students with disability labels. For these students, teachers should also rely on IEP team members to check the relevance of curriculum decisions with individuals who know the student in different ways, including the parent and related service personnel. Using a collaborative decision-making model allows for multiple perspectives for the most comprehensive picture of the abilities and needs of the student.

Will the student with disabilities be working at grade level?

Students with disabilities are assigned to a grade level based on their chronological age. This provides an opportunity for children to have peers to serve as role models and an opportunity for peer friendship development. A student's chronological age may or may not coincide with his or her assessed or perceived mental age. A student who is nine years old will be placed in a fourth grade class regardless of whether he or she reads at a sixth grade level, a first grade level, or is presently a non-reader. This concept is critically important in assisting students to develop an age-appropriate repertoire of skills.

Students with disabilities are assigned to a grade level based on their chronological age.

The intent of inclusion is to support all students in settings with their chronological age appropriate peers and with curriculum and instruction that accommodates their range of needs and abilities. Some students (e.g., students with serious social/emotional disabilities) may be achieving at or above grade level in all content areas, while other students (e.g., students with specific learning disabilities) may be achieving at or above grade level in some content areas but below grade level in other areas. Some students will be achieving below grade level in all academic areas, and some may have goals which do not focus on specific academic skills but which prioritize basic skills in areas such as mobility and communication. All of these needs can be met within an age appropriate general education classroom setting if the teacher is given appropriate support.

How does a student with disabilities fit into the grade level curriculum?

Students with disabilities will be educated based on their needs, skills, and interests in a manner similar to their peers. Students with disabilities will be exposed to all aspects of the curriculum and classroom activities yet will have specific expectations based on their individual needs.

Unlike their peers without disabilities, students with disabilities have help in determining their needs because of the blueprint laid out in the IEP. Each student's IEP will address general goals and specific objectives that the student is expected to achieve. These objectives are considered by the teacher and infused into curricular units based upon academic skills to be developed and/or broader skills to be practiced and reinforced within given classroom activities. In addition, access to mastering the curriculum objectives is achieved by modifying instructional strategies and adapting the curriculum.

How will I meet the individual learning needs of the included student?

To enhance the participation and contribution of students with disabilities and to meet the individualized objectives outlined in the student's IEP, the school site team may need to make decisions to modify the core curriculum. Adaptations or modifications to the curriculum can be viewed as any adjustment in the goals, instruction, environment, or materials used to support student participation and learning (Udvari-Solner, 1992). There are many models of curriculum modification available in the educational literature, but most models address how the content is delivered, how it is mastered, or the way in which the student participates. Based upon these available models and also upon observations of teachers in schools, the following curriculum modification model may be useful to teachers as they include students with disabilities. Teachers are encouraged to consider each level when making curricular decisions for the students with disabilities in their classrooms.

For many students with disabilities, curricular content, classroom activities, and daily routines will require no modification.

♦ **As is—no modifications are necessary.** For many students with disabilities, curricular content, classroom activities, and daily routines will require no modification. The curriculum can be presented as it is usually presented to all students. For example, Eduardo requires no additional assistance to activate his wheelchair to move from the door of his classroom to the morning circle area. He also requires no additional assistance to respond with a loud vocalization to indicate his presence in class when the teacher takes attendance. Tameka requires no assistance when participating in math activities and, based on her strong memory skills, is a sought after partner in social studies activities based on vocabulary mastery.

♦ **Provide physical assistance.** Some students with disabilities will require physical assistance to more fully participate in class activities. This assistance can be provided by peers, teaching staff, or related service personnel. For example, Claire may need a peer to help her discriminate between the hot and cold faucets in the girl's restroom. A peer may place Claire's hand on the appropriate faucet to get her started washing her hands. Tameka may ask a peer to walk to the nurse's office with her to take her medication, while Eduardo needs a trained adult to help him eat with his gastro intestinal tube.

◆ **Use material adaptations.** Teachers typically use a variety of instructional materials to enhance student learning and students with disabilities may require modifications of these materials. Materials may be changed or substituted to better match the preferred learning styles of students with disabilities. For example, Thang's journal writing is enhanced when he uses a mind map to compose his thoughts. Claire benefits from raised glue outlines on art projects to indicate the edges of shapes. Tameka is most successful when the number of items on a page is reduced and when enlarged print is used. For Eduardo, a magnetic lap board allows him to participate in cooperative groups in the afternoon when he is positioned out of his chair on a bean bag. The board allows him to hold materials for the group.

◆ **Select and use multi-level outcomes.** Teachers know that all students have different ways of knowing, demonstrate different intelligences, and learn at different rates. Students with disabilities share these characteristics with their nondisabled peers. To best match the individual objectives of students with disabilities with the core curriculum, teachers may need to vary the goals and objectives of lessons. For example, while some students may be working on grammar and speaking in front of the class during sharing time, Eduardo may bring in several Polaroid pictures showing what he did over the weekend instead of orally describing his weekend as his nondisabled peers do. The modified outcome allows Eduardo to participate while also working on his IEP objectives. During sustained silent reading, Claire may listen to a favorite story on tape, using headphones and a walkman. While she is not engaging in reading, she is working on a related goal to attend to a story for longer and longer periods of time. Using a walkman is helping her to reach this goal. (**Note:** These examples include material adaptations as well).

◆ **Select and use goals outside the content area.** As suggested previously, different students will have different objectives across content areas. When most students are working on the academic content of a particular subject, some students with disabilities may be working on a basic skill within that content area. Within academic lessons, students have many opportunities to work on developing basic skills while they may or may not be working on meeting academic goals within the content area. For example, Eduardo may be working on keeping his head up and responding to his name during a cooperative group lesson on creating a picture book for

Teachers typically use a variety of instructional materials to enhance student learning and students with disabilities may require modifications of these materials.

The Very Hungry Caterpillar (Carle, 1987). He would have multiple opportunities to work on these skills while passing materials to peers or while responding to the groups' pictures. For Tameka, during a literature discussion group, her primary objective is to monitor her tone of voice, attend to the speaker, and stay on the topic. In both of these examples, the students are working on basic skills needs within an academic lesson. Basic skills needs such as these require that student have multiple opportunities to work on them across content areas and settings to ensure generalization of these skills.

Will every activity we do in class have to be adapted every day?

As discussed in the previous section, there will be many activities in which students with disabilities can participate without any specific adaptations and other activities that will need to be specifically modified to allow student participation and enhance learning opportunities. There are also specific daily activities that occur regularly for which accommodations can be determined and offered. For example, journal writing takes place in Claire's class for 20 minutes every morning. Claire's support team has decided that she can choose between drawing a story, dictating a three-sentence story to a peer and then copying the sentences herself, cutting and pasting a story with magazine pictures, or creating a story with rubber stamps and ink. Although journal time must be modified for Claire, it is not necessary to make specific adaptations each day. The team has developed pre-determined choices for Claire that are easily available within the daily activity of journal writing.

Tameka also has routine choices within daily activities. During the daily activity of community circle, students are expected to share current events from the news or from their own lives and then participate in a question and answer dialogue about topics presented. Presently, Tameka is unable to sit for a long period of time to participate in discussion activities. The teacher, in conjunction with the support team, may determine that Tameka can choose to bring something with her to community circle in order to help sustain her ability to sit with the group, such as a book to read or a pad to draw on. If that is considered too distracting to the teacher, or to that particular group of students, Tameka may be expected to participate in the group for the first or last five minutes, learning to share and ask or answer a question. The rest of the time she may be involved in an activity geared toward her IEP objectives. Over the course of the year, the amount of time in which Tameka participates with her peers in the group is expected to increase.

There are also specific daily activities that occur regularly for which accommodations can be determined and offered.

In addition to activities that occur regularly, most teachers utilize specific or common instructional routines within lessons to present content and provide opportunities for content mastery. Adaptations can also be designed to fit these typical instructional routines found in any classroom. For example, social studies lessons might typically consist of presenting new or review information through teacher lecture, checking for understanding of that information by an oral question and answer period, mastering content through a cooperative group activity and then demonstrating knowledge in an independent paper and pencil task. A science lesson may consist of the same basic instructional routines, although with different content.

When a teacher considers involving a student with disabilities in these instructional routines, it is helpful to examine the routines in terms of both content and activities. The team may decide that a student is more successful during all teacher lecture times if he or she is allowed to write in a journal or draw in a scratch paper pad while listening or waiting for the next activity. If note-taking is to occur, an easy accommodation is to present the student with several index cards on which key points of the lecture, or an outline of the lecture being given, are printed, allowing the student to copy words or fill in blanks from the lecture. A successful strategy for determining a student's role in a cooperative group activity may simply be a reminder to peers of one or two of the student's IEP goals as they are determining roles within the cooperative groups. It may be that for some students, all paper and pencil tasks need to be specifically adapted either in advance or on the spot to meet his or her needs.

When a teacher considers involving a student with disabilities into these instructional routines, it is helpful to examine the routines in terms of both content and activities.

Examining the routines that occur across the curriculum can provide the team with an opportunity to develop strategies or prepare supportive materials in advance, regardless of the specific content to be covered. Some of the routines outlined for Tameka include the following:

◆ Anytime silent reading is expected, Tameka is instructed to read quietly for a 5 or 10-minute period of time. She may then quietly walk in a circle around the room two times as a physical activity break, and may listen to books on tape with her walkman.

◆ During class question and answer periods, Tameka is reminded to raise her hand and is then called upon early and asked to make two statements related to the topic. A peer then writes the topic and her statements on a piece of paper, and she copies that answer in her own writing.

◆ During teacher lecture times, Tameka is given something to physically manipulate at her desk, such as clay or a Rubik's cube.

◆ During long periods of independent writing tasks, Tameka can access the computer.

◆ During free choice times or classroom centers, Tameka is reinforced for choosing an activity and staying with it for five minutes before changing activities.

Teachers have, at times, expressed concern that although the adapted materials they create, or are provided with by a member of the team, are helpful and relevant, the adaptation supports only one part of the lesson. For example, receiving an adapted worksheet from the inclusion support teacher helps the student for that segment of the activity, but it is not helpful for the ten minutes spent by the teacher explaining the concept to be practiced on the worksheet. Devising strategies for classroom instructional routines will help identify the activities for which specific content is to be adapted but will also ensure that the student is successfully engaged throughout each component of the lesson.

Some decisions regarding adaptations will need to be made for specific lessons or activities to meet the child's individuals needs and to enhance participation.

How will I adapt specific lessons or activities?

Some decisions regarding adaptations will need to be made for specific lessons or activities to meet the child's individual needs and to enhance participation. The following Classroom Activity Analysis Worksheet adapted from Neary & Mintun (1991) is a helpful tool for the general education teacher and inclusion support teacher to complete and use to determine specific adaptations for particular activities or lessons. In the first column, Classroom Activity Steps, the behaviors expected by any student are listed. In the second column, Student Skills, the behaviors demonstrated by the student with disabilities are listed and described. The point of this comparison is to determine where specific adaptations may be needed. In the third column, the Specific Adaptations are listed using the categories described in this chapter as a reference (e.g., as is, provide physical assistance, use material adaptations, select and use multi-level outcomes, and select and use goals outside the content area). The final column, Skills in Need of Instruction, allows the general education teacher and the inclusion support teacher to target particular behaviors for direct or specific instruction. A completed Classroom Activity Analysis Worksheet for Thang is presented on the following page. A blank form is provided for you on page 42.

Classroom Activity Analysis Worksheet

Name of Student: Thang

Date: November 15, 1995

Teacher: M. Cook and J. Smith

Activity: Social Studies: Research Reports on Ancient Greece and Rome

Classroom Activity Steps	Student Skills	Specific Adaptations	Skills in Need of Instruction
1. Teacher gives directions.	Has difficulty with verbal directions. Does not maintain attention to task.	Teacher writes information on the board.	Follow verbal directions.
2. Students share outlines of their reports in small groups.	Same as peers.	None necessary.	None.
3. Students take notes from reference materials.	Has difficulty reading materials independently. Cannot locate main points.	Takes notes from high-lighted material (prepared by aid).	Locate main points. Increase reading comprehension.
4. Students write individual reports.	Has difficulty writing. Copies without understanding.	Dictates information to a parent volunteer. Thang edits material.	Increase vocabulary in content area. Use correct spelling and punctuation.
5. Students share progress in whole group setting.	Same as peers.	None necessary.	None.

Classroom Activity Analysis Worksheet

Name of Student:

Teacher:

Activity:

Date:

Classroom Activity Steps	Student Skills	Specific Adaptations	Skills in Need of Instruction

Instructional
Considerations

How do I provide effective instruction for the range of diverse learners in my class?

Once teachers have decided on the curricular content their students with diverse learning needs will master, the focus shifts to the ways teachers will introduce information as well as provide their students with opportunities to apply those concepts. Just as what to teach varies based upon student diversity, how to teach varies as well. Teachers who use a range of instructional strategies in presenting material and facilitating student interaction with new concepts will have the greatest success in meeting the range of student needs.

In the past, traditional elementary school practices often reflected the view of children as empty containers to be filled with knowledge. Current cognitive research on how children learn has led teachers to develop and deliver curriculum that builds upon children's natural talent and propensity to discover knowledge about their world (Tharp & Gallimore, 1988). Learning by doing (Dewey, 1956) is a value long held by educators to increase student participation and learning in schools. Simply, active students learn more. The instruc-

> Just as what to teach varies based upon student diversity, how to teach varies as well.

tional strategies a teacher selects and the instructional arrangements that are used should encourage students to be active participants in the learning process.

Every student, including students with disabilities, brings unique strengths and challenges to schools and these strengths, challenges, and experiences should be recognized and nurtured (Carbo, 1995). While schools have typically met the needs of students who have linguistic and mathematical intelligences, large numbers of students with and without disabilities demonstrate intelligence in other areas. Building upon these student characteristics and experiences, teachers can provide students with active learning opportunities which emphasize interaction, function, and meaning.

One way to build on these individual student characteristics is to attend to the multiple intelligences as described previously.

One way to build on these individual student characteristics is to attend to the multiple intelligences as described previously. The information about a student's areas of intelligence can help determine a student's learning style. Personal learning style refers to those strategies a student uses to acquire new concepts and skills.

By attending to these varied strengths, teachers can recognize and use the many talents diverse learners in their classrooms bring to school when considering the best instructional arrangements and strategies to use. For example, Eduardo is talented in the musical area, and his peers are impressed with his ability to activate the tape recorder with his cheek switch during music time. Based upon his mother's suggestion, the teacher allows classical music to play softly in the background to assist him to attend and remain alert throughout the day. The members of Claire's school site team have recognized her interpersonal area of intelligence and strength. Claire's teacher recognizes and encourages her ability to mediate conflicts among peers by using partner activities and cooperative learning activities often. Tameka's greatest strength is in the logical/mathematical area. She is often called upon to assist peers when new math or logic problems are introduced. Her teacher recognizes this gift and facilitates Tameka's helping other students by explaining difficult concepts in language they understand. Thang is a strong spatial learner and understands concepts best when he is allowed to draw them. He has contributed to his classmates' understanding of various geography lessons by his illustrations.

Do students with disabilities have to work in one-to-one settings?

In any given day, students will have the opportunity to learn in different configurations. They may work independently, spend time in small groups, or work as a class, depending on the curricular topic or the activity. During any of these arrangements, a student should participate in activities that allow him to make progress on the goals designed to meet his individual needs. The practice of providing students with disabilities with all instruction in one-to-one arrangements has, in fact, led to adult/peer dependency for many students. Reliance on this arrangement leads students with disabilities to become used to being told what to do and when to do it. Therefore, these students do not learn to respond to natural learning conditions.

What are considerations for the student with disabilities during whole class instruction?

When whole class instruction is used, students are often expected to receive the same content at the same rate (Udvari-Solner, 1994). It is important to caution against overusing this strategy as individual needs and strengths of many students can be overlooked. This, in turn, can lead to an increase in disruptive behavior if students are not meaningfully engaged in the lesson. Some elements a teacher may need to attend to in regards to these arrangements include the following:

Typically, there will be many opportunities for students to work independently throughout the school day.

◆ the student's academic readiness for the material—is this material appropriate for the student's learning level?

◆ the student's attention span—can the student attend for the expected length of the lesson?

◆ the student's communication skills—can the student comprehend what is being taught and/or can the student provide a response in a discussion?

It may also be necessary to provide adaptations or accommodations to increase the student's success during whole class instruction.

What are considerations for the student with disabilities during independent work time?

Typically, there will be many opportunities for students to work independently throughout the school day. Considerations for students with disabilities might also include the following:

◆ familiarity with the task—does the student know what to do?

◆ need for assistance—can the student ask for help?

◆ length of work time—can the student maintain attention?

What are considerations for the student with disabilities when the students work with partners?

Many benefits result when students work in a collaborative manner. When planning for students with disabilities in partner settings teachers might consider the following: (1) choosing partners with similar interests; (2) choosing partners who will benefit from the pairing; (3) establishing a reciprocal relationship (where both partners learn something); (4) helping students guide instruction rather than telling the answers; and (5) changing partners for different subjects areas or activities.

What are considerations for the student with disabilities when the students are working in cooperative groups?

When compared with individualistic or competitive learning situations, several researchers have demonstrated the positive effects of cooperative learning for students with disabilities. In these studies and in others, students with disabilities have demonstrated improved academic achievement and social acceptance.

Simply placing children in small group configurations will not guarantee that they will be able to work cooperatively. In order for children to be successful in cooperative group settings, they must learn the social skills that guide group interactions. When teachers identify those skills necessary for working in a group and provide instruction on the development of these behaviors, students will be more aware and effective group members. An activity for illustrating cooperative group skills is included on page 47

Simply placing children in small group configurations will not guarantee that they will be able to work cooperatively.

Help Your Group

Once you are in a group, there are several things you can do to help accomplish group goals.

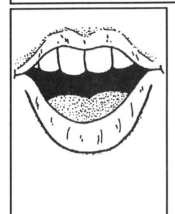

Contribute ideas to the group.

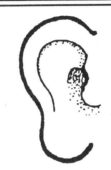

Listen carefully for ideas from others.

Help the group make good decisions.

Cooperate rather than compete.

Solve problems in a calm manner.

Fill in the last box with your own idea.

Reprinted from TCM 652 Cooperative Learning Actvities for Language Arts, *Teacher Created Materials, 1995*

Cooperative learning activities may be structured in different ways based on the curricular area, the specific task, and the needs of the students involved. Particular considerations for students with disabilities might include the following: determination of an active role for the student in the group, recognizing the need for the student to be involved in the lesson (as opposed to observing the lesson), considering the length of the activity with respect to the student's ability to attend or remain on task, addressing the student's communication needs and skills for the lesson, and analyzing the adaptations necessary for the student to be a contributing group member.

Are there specific instructional strategies I can use for students with disabilities?

There are many instructional aides and strategies that may be successful for students with or without disabilities. It will be useful for the general educator to be familiar with the specific systematic instructional strategies that have historically been used in special education so that he or she can use such strategies with the student with disabilities. Many of these are useful with nondisabled students who may need more intensive instruction in certain areas of the curriculum. Teachers can assist their students to access the curriculum by encouraging students to use the following learning aids.

Graphic organizers such as outlines, brainstorming, mind maps, and story maps help some students put their thinking on paper before they begin writing a more comprehensive draft. Having the opportunity to generate a list or to record related words and phrases may alleviate some of the pressure associated with more formal writing tasks. Organizing the material in advance allows students to write in a more logical, structured manner and facilitates the completion of a fluent, sequential piece of writing. Checklists may also be used to encourage students to monitor the necessary components to be included in a written assignment.

It may be helpful for some students to have cue cards on their desks to assist them with vocabulary related to curricular content. When studying geography for example, Thang may need to have a picture of a globe with the lines of latitude and longitude identified and labeled in different colors. This strategy would allow Thang to follow the class discussion and would provide a readily available resource if he needed to review the related terms or concepts. Providing multiple opportunities to draw information as an alternative to writing may also encourage students to assimilate the material into a picture that may be more easily learned and remembered.

Students who need support with spelling may find personal dictionaries, word banks, and study lists to be of value. These strategies are most helpful if students are focusing on the words that they encounter most often in their own reading and writing. Students may need multiple opportunities for spelling practice and review and should be encouraged to find the strategy that works best for them. As in other content areas, it is important that students recognize that the ability to locate the correct information is as valuable as knowing the answer.

Other more specialized strategies include positive reinforcement, task analysis, prompting, shaping, chaining, and fading. Each of these strategies will be briefly described and an example provided.

Positive reinforcement is a concept that is very familiar to most teachers. Catching students when they are good is a powerful way to reinforce and thus increase desirable behavior. For students with disabilities, positive reinforcement is often combined with other instructional strategies to assist a student to engage in or learn a skill or concept. For example, Claire's teacher uses Sparkle Awards in his class when children are caught engaged in a kind and helpful act. Children are recognized and thanked, and then they write their name on a strip of paper that is then attached to a paper chain that is hung around the room. When the chain stretches the entire length of the room, the class is treated to a pizza party. While this strategy was originally developed with Claire in mind, it has been helpful with all students to increase acts of kindness. Teachers are advised to systematically monitor the reinforcement and behavior to check how effective a particular strategy is for the specific student and the targeted behavior.

Task analysis is a method by which tasks, skills, and concepts are broken down into smaller instructional units to facilitate student learning. While this method has traditionally been used in special education, many general educators use this approach to present curriculum to a diverse group of learners. For example, Eduardo's teacher was assisted by his inclusion support teacher to analyze how Eduardo might more fully participate in jump rope at recess. In thinking about the steps of the activity, they agreed that while he could not jump, he seemed to enjoy listening to the rhyming songs the children sang as they jumped rope. When the two teachers put their heads together and thought about what part of the activity Eduardo could do, they came up with the idea of attaching the rope to his wheelchair. This allowed him to be a part of the activity that he seemed to enjoy.

> Catching students when they are good is a powerful way to reinforce and thus increase desirable behavior.

Prompting involves specific guidance and instructional assistance to facilitate students acquiring new skills. Prompts may take the form of cues, which are used to provide instructional information to a student before a skill is performed. Prompts may also be used as corrections which let a student know that the skill or concept demonstrated was incorrect and needs to be attempted in a different way. For example, there are many opportunities during a typical day when teachers can assist students to learn from the natural cues around them. For example, after lunch, the lunch aide prompts Tameka to remember what to do with her lunch tray. Tameka typically jumps up and leaves the table when she sees her peers finishing their lunches. The aide asks her, "What else do you need to do?" When the question is posed in this way, it allows Tameka to think about her behavior before she acts and then to respond appropriately by taking her tray to the window.

Chaining is another procedure that can be used to develop new behaviors and skills.

Shaping begins with positive reinforcement of the closest approximation of the desired behavior and then builds on slight changes in the behavior toward the targeted goal or behavior. Many different behaviors that are currently not in the student's repertoire can be developed by using shaping procedures. For example, Eduardo can be taught by the inclusion support teacher to touch his peers on their forearms when he wants their attention instead of pulling at their clothes. At first any light touch to the arm or chest can be reinforced, and then additional reinforcement can be contingent upon touching the forearm area only.

Chaining is another procedure that can be used to develop new behaviors and skills. Chaining involves breaking a target behavior down into its smallest parts in order to teach the parts one at a time. Chaining begins with a task analysis of the skill or behavior and would be used with positive reinforcement and prompting. For example, Claire learned to erase the chalkboard when the task was broken into several steps. The aide taught her a couple of steps at a time and then helped her to put all the pieces together to complete the task in the correct sequence.

Fading is an important instructional strategy to use when intense prompting has been used to teach a student a particular skill or behavior. Many students with disabilities quickly become prompt dependent; that is, they cannot perform the skill or complete the behavior unless the prompt is present. Any use of prompting must also include a systematic plan to reduce the student's dependence on prompts and to teach the student to respond to the natural cues to sustain the acquired skill. Fading is essentially the removing of prompts used for instruction slowly and systematically. In the preceding example, the school site team would make sure that Claire had learned the skill of erasing the board before removing the prompts provided by the instructional assistant. The more visible prompts are removed first (i.e., physical assistance) and then later the more subtle prompts (i.e., any gestures or verbal reminders). The goal of fading is to assist the student to attend to and learn from the natural cues that are available in his/her environment.

The best way to learn about these strategies is to consult with special education professionals in the district, former teachers of a particular student, the student's parent, and/or the student him or herself. Learning what has been successful in the past will help save valuable instructional time at the beginning of each year. In addition, it is important to know what strategies have been unsuccessful in the past so that time is not wasted.

In addition to considering instructional arrangements and strategies, there are other instructional issues a teacher must address to facilitate the successful inclusion of students with a range of abilities and needs. These considerations include classroom management, individual behavior support plans, physical classroom arrangements, and provisions for students with medical needs.

What is the best system for classroom management?

An important first step in any classroom management plan is the establishment of the classroom as a community which provides students with a sense of belonging. The importance of a caring classroom community has been previously mentioned in the introductory chapter of this book.

Two strategies that can help to build a sense of community are circles of friends and tribes. Circles of friends involves bringing together a group of students to meet on a regular and ongoing basis. This concept began with students with disabilities as the focus (Forest & Lusthaus, 1989) but is an appropriate strategy for all students. By using this strategy teachers can arrange opportunities that allow students with and without disabilities to interact with one another and to become more involved in each other's social network. A teacher usually facilitates this group, and in the beginning it may be quite formal with a specific agenda in mind. As students become comfortable with this process, the meetings usually become more informal, with peers often assuming the role of the facilitator and the focus changing from the needs of one student to other students' needs.

An important first step in any classroom management plan is the establishment of the classroom as a community which provides students with a sense of belonging.

Tribes (Gibbs, 1995) is a systematic process to increase self-esteem, social responsibility, and academic achievement in students. Fundamental to this process is the belief that children who maintain long-term membership in supportive classroom peer groups will enhance their self-images and demonstrate more responsible behavior and increased motivation toward academic achievement. Tribes are composed of groups of five to six students who meet regularly throughout the school year to promote a sense of belonging and caring. A sequence of group activities facilitated by the classroom teacher develops trust and respect among students. As tribes become supportive working groups, they are used for problem solving and decision making through peer interaction.

In classroom communities, the sense of shared responsibility and supporting one another is enhanced by classroom management strategies that include students as decision makers in that community. Students are encouraged to become thoughtful, self-directed, concerned about others, and committed to their classroom, school, and neighborhood community. One strategy that is particularly successful in inclusive classrooms is described as a democratic classroom.

Disruptive or other problematic behaviors often occur due to the classroom ecology or classroom environment.

What is a democratic classroom?

Dinkmeyer, McKay, and Dinkmeyer (1980) identify four guidelines for designing a democratic classroom where the emphasis is on self-discipline. First, establish a climate of mutuality and respect where all members of the classroom share equal status and contributions are encouraged. Second, provide support to the students by focusing on the students' assets and strengths and accentuating their positive traits. Third, provide students a role in decision making by acknowledging their opinions and choices regarding topics of study, projects, bulletin boards, and other classroom issues. Finally, help students develop self-discipline by offering them consistent, logical, fully understood guidelines for their behavior. By emphasizing appropriate behavior choices in this type of classroom, disruptive behavior is often reduced.

Should there be special behavior rules in a classroom that includes students with disabilities?

Special behavior rules will not be required because behavior rules that are appropriate and helpful for students with disabilities are also appropriate and helpful for students without disabilities. Disruptive or other problematic behaviors often occur due to the classroom ecology or classroom environment. For example, competitive classroom environments can lead some students to feel they are not measuring up and are an academic failures. These students may then act out or, conversely, withdraw from the situation. Changes to the classroom ecology that lead to such reactions can therefore limit disruptive or other problematic behaviors and assist students to develop appropriate and constructive skills.

The most important rule in any classroom is that all people are to be treated with dignity and respect. Students must be given opportunities to practice interacting with each other in supportive ways and will need guidance from teachers in learning specific strategies for problem solving and conflict resolution. Support from teachers to develop strong communication skills is essential in building a classroom community and reducing the need for behavior problems. Students who do not have strong verbal communication skills or are uncomfortable talking in front of peers may choose to participate by writing or drawing their ideas. A student with an augmentative communication board, like Eduardo, can be given specific pictures to choose from that might help express his feelings or thoughts on a particular issue.

The most important rule in any classroom is that all people are to be treated with dignity and respect.

Teaching students to develop and utilize conflict management skills is an important part of classroom management. Fostering conflict resolution among students, as opposed to being between teacher and student, encourages students to take responsibility for conflict resolution rather than relying on teacher intervention. Techniques that help promote conflict resolution skills for students include storytelling, effective listening, role playing, class and small group discussions, and activities aimed at reducing stereotypes and increasing appreciation of individual differences (Jubala, Bishop, & Falvey, 1995). A language arts lesson that encourages children to problem solve is What Would You Do? located on pages 54 through 56.

In addition, structuring the classroom environment to provide positive, cooperative relationships through activities, projects, and shared responsibilities helps promote positive interaction opportunities among peers. Through carefully planned curriculum opportunities, a teacher can provide activities that will promote a feeling of success and accomplishment for all students. Students can be encouraged to work at their own levels while continuing to be perceived as valuable, contributing members of the class. In a classroom where a strong sense of community and belonging are fostered, all members of the class are celebrated for successes at any level.

What Would You Do?

For this activity, you will need to be in groups of 3, 4, or 6.

Cut apart the cards on this page, page 55, and page 56. Stack them in a deck with the title card on top. Distribute the question cards by dealing them in equal amounts to all group members. Take turns reading and answering the question cards you hold. The player who has the card gets to answer the question on it. Continue playing until all cards have been read and answered.

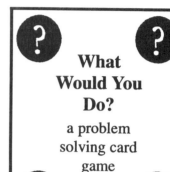

What Would You Do?

a problem solving card game

You do not like the television show your family has chosen to watch.  *What would you do?*	Your best friend did not want to play with you at recess. *What would you do?*	Somebody broke a window at school. You know who did it. *What would you do?*
You got out of bed and tripped on your skateboard. *What would you do?*	You ate the last piece of cake without asking. Your mother asks you if you know where the cake is. *What would you do?*	Your teacher tells you that you are singing too loud during the music time. *What would you do?*

Reprinted from TCM 353 Literature Activities for Reluctant Readers, *Teacher Created Materials, 1991*

What Would You Do? *(cont.)*

For this activity, you will need to be in groups of 3, 4, or 6.

Another child on the playground pushes you down. It really hurts.  *What would you do?*	Your little sister scribbles all over your art project.  *What would you do?*	You drop a sweater into the sink while the water is running.  *What would you do?*
You have had a terrible day. Nothing is going right.  *What would you do?*	The clerk gives you too much change when you pay for your ice cream. *What would you do?*	You do not want to share a toy with your friend. Your friend will leave if you don't share. *What would you do?*
Your mother serves you lima beans for dinner. You hate lima beans.  *What would you do?*	A new girl comes into your class. She doesn't know anybody and is very shy. She sits next to you. *What would you do?*	You accidentally drop your dad's calculator. It isn't working now. *What would you do?*

Reprinted from TCM 353 Literature Activities for Reluctant Readers, *Teacher Created Materials, 1991*

What Would You Do? *(cont.)*

Cut these cards apart. See page 54 for activity directions.

Your older sister's friends come over to your house. They do not want you to play with them, but you really want to.  *What would you do?*	There is no dessert in your lunch box. Every child sitting around you has dessert. 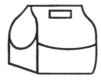 *What would you do?*	Everyone else in your family gets the tennis shoes they want. You can't. They only have plain white ones in your size.  *What would you do?*
A kid in your class keeps calling you names.  *What would you do?*	Someone at lunch took your sandwich and played kickball with it.  *What would you do?*	Your brother calls you a crybaby.  *What would you do?*
Your teacher times you out for talking out of turn in class. But, you weren't the only one.  *What would you do?*	You really want a remote control race car. You can see one on a bench in the park. No people are near it.  *What would you do?*	One of the children in your class took your new set of colored pencils and won't give them back.  *What would you do?*

Reprinted from TCM 353 Literature Activities for Reluctant Readers, *Teacher Created Materials, 1991*

What about the student who continually struggles with his or her behavior?

Even in a classroom where self-discipline is fostered and problems are addressed in a logical and supportive manner, there may be some students who often have difficulty choosing appropriate behaviors. There may be a range of student behaviors exhibited in a diverse classroom. Most students will respond to a well-organized, positive atmosphere with rich curricular opportunities and effective instructional strategies. However, some students may continue to be unsuccessful in completing assignments on time, may have difficulty remaining on task during classroom activities, or may even exhibit disruptive, aggressive or self-injurious behavior.

With students who have ongoing behavioral difficulties it is important to realize that behavior management plans that rely on punishing the inappropriate behaviors are likely to be ineffective in the long run. If strategies such as writing names on the chalkboard or losing lunch or recess time were effective strategies, we would not continue to see behavior problems in the same children year after year.

For students who have significant or continual behavior problems, it is necessary to determine why the student is doing what it is he or she is doing. This process, called a functional analysis (Carr, Robinson, & Palumbo, 1990), presumes that every behavior serves a purpose and that by exhibiting these inappropriate behaviors, a child is communicating an important message and/or getting an important need met. The intent is, then, for teachers, with support from parents, school counselors, psychologists, and/or special educators, to determine what that need is and then teach the child an appropriate way to get that need met.

How can I determine what the purpose of a behavior is?

Often the purpose, or function, of a behavior can be determined by examining the events in a child's life through his or her eyes. Try to determine if a child might be bored, frustrated, lonely, or frightened for some reason, unable to communicate needs, assert him or herself, interact with peers, or understand a task. Examine when the child is successful and behaving appropriately. What is different between those times and the more difficult times? Consulting with the child and his or her family might also give a teacher insight into the reason for the problem behavior.

If the function of the behavior does not become clear after some initial observations and brainstorming, there are specific strategies that

> Most students will respond to a well organized, positive atmosphere with rich curricular opportunities and effective instructional strategies.

57

can lead to more sophisticated data collection to pinpoint what the function of a particular behavior might be. Bishop and Jubala (1995) present an introduction to some of those strategies and how they can be effectively used by families and educators.

How does knowing the function of a behavior help change the problem?

Once the function of the behavior is identified, the teacher can begin teaching the student appropriate ways to get his or her needs met. For example, if the function of a behavior is to get attention from peers, the teacher can provide classroom activities that teach appropriate social interaction skills. By learning to initiate and sustain an interaction with a peer, the student may no longer have to be aggressive to gain the peer's attention. Tameka's school site team was able to determine that she exhibited many of her behavioral outbursts during transition periods. The team determined that the function of her behavior might be to say that she was confused about what would be happening next. To prevent this confusion, the teacher would give a five-minute warning to the class that an activity was about to be completed. At that time a designated peer would quietly tell Tameka where she was going and what she would be doing next. In addition, it was determined that Tameka would be taught to raise her hand and ask a question or make a statement that she was worried about what to do next in order to help her be less reliant on an artificial built-in structure in the future.

> Once the function of the behavior is identified, the teacher can begin teaching the student appropriate ways to get his or her needs met.

The goal of the behavior intervention team is to teach a student those skills which are valued and socially accepted in inclusion. Many educators simply try to stop an inappropriate behavior without determining why the student is engaging in that behavior. Although a program to stop a behavior may seem to be successful in the short term, it is likely that a substitute behavior that is equally inappropriate will be exhibited to get needs met. By acknowledging a student's needs and teaching appropriate skills, teachers can see long term success in behavior change.

How can a teacher determine the function of a behavior and develop a plan while teaching an entire class of students?

A student who has severe and ongoing behavior challenges will need specific support from the school site team or professionals specifically trained in the functional analysis process. Although the teacher is expected to provide information and to be a fully contributing member of the team, it is not reasonable to expect any one person to be successful in this effective but time consuming process. The teacher will need support in collecting functional analysis data, analyzing that data, and building a support plan for teaching new behaviors within the context of the general education classroom.

Shouldn't students with behavior problems be served in special education classrooms until their behavior improves?

Sometimes students with disabilities exhibit behavior problems simply because they are in a segregated environment. A classroom full of students with disabilities may not provide any appropriate role models and may only serve to enhance a student's repertoire of inappropriate behaviors. If a student is put into a classroom for students with behavior problems, he or she will live up to that expectation and will successfully exhibit behavior problems! Some students will resent being segregated from typical peers and will increase their inappropriate behaviors as a form of protest.

> Sometimes students with disabilities exhibit behavior problems simply because they are in a segregated environment.

Essentially, students who have challenging behaviors need to have support in changing their behavior. That support should be provided in the most appropriate setting, i.e., the general education classroom. It is not acceptable for a student to hit another student in a general education classroom. Neither is it appropriate for a student to hit a student in a special education classroom. The point is that a student must learn to resolve problems without hitting. An inclusive setting with support for the teacher can provide that student the opportunity to learn the necessary coping, communication, and/or social skills to change behavior patterns and to be a productive member of his/her community.

What about physical accommodations in the classroom?

It is necessary to consider a child's physical needs within the classroom, as well as academic needs, to promote successful inclusion. For students who are easily distracted, a desk near the door or window may not be a wise choice. Students who use wheelchairs may need aisles between desks to be wider in order to be able to move about the room safely and comfortably. Students who have hearing impairments may need to sit facing the teacher and the chalkboard in order to more effectively use incoming sensory information (e.g., see the teacher's lips while he talks). Students with visual impairments may need to sit in the front row and may be more successful viewing white on black transparencies.

What adaptations will I need to make for a student with health and medical needs?

The health and medical needs of students with disabilities is often of concern to school personnel. In reality, schools regularly make adaptations for students with medical needs. For example, a child may need to visit the school office twice a day to receive his medication which is kept locked in the office. A student who has a heart condition may need frequent rests during physical education. Other medical needs may require more intensive support. If a child has medical or health needs, such as Eduardo does, school staff must be specifically assigned and trained to care for those needs. There are several strategies that can be used to ensure that there is effective care for a child's significant medical needs. A nurse can be assigned to the school site where the child with significant medical needs attends or a health aide who is also a licensed vocational or registered nurse can be assigned to support the child in school. It is also necessary to have emergency plans in place so that school staff and peers can respond appropriately to any medical incident, such as a grand mal seizure. Even for routine care, it is important that fully knowledgeable medical staff, such as the student's pediatrician, be consulted regarding how to best address medical issues as they arise.

The health and medical needs of students with disabilities is often of concern to school personnel.

Putting It All Together

The intent of this book is to provide teachers and other professionals with strategies and resources they can use to develop and implement successful inclusive education for students with and without disabilities. But even with such information, it may still be hard to "see" how inclusion could work. In this section of the book, descriptions of typical days for two of the students that you have read about in previous sections are presented. The purpose of providing these portraits is to give the reader a sense of how inclusion looks and how the individual supports and resources are infused into a student's day.

Two planning tools are described first. Teachers have reported each to be useful in thinking about and planning for the educational program for students with disabilities in inclusive settings. In the IEP chapter the reader was introduced to the Full Inclusion Scheduling Matrix. This matrix can guide the team in deciding what individual needs can be met throughout the scheduled activities in the general education class. An elaborated Full Inclusion Support Planning Grid, based upon the scheduling matrix, is described below.

The Full Inclusion Support Planning Grid was originally developed in conjunction with a resource specialist teacher and a first grade teacher as they collaborated to include a student with disabilities.

In this section of the book, descriptions of typical days for two of the students that you have read about in previous sections are presented.

61

These teachers described it as the primary communication tool for the members of the school team. The class schedule is written down the left hand side of the matrix and individual student objectives from his/her IEP are written across the top of the grid. The team decides what class periods provide the opportunity to work on each of the objectives. The key at the bottom of the grid allows the team to designate both the type of curriculum modification for each objective and class period, as well as to identify who will be responsible for providing the assistance and support.

The Full Inclusion Support Planning Menu guides the team in deciding what supports are needed for effective inclusion efforts. This menu was originally developed by a general education teacher to maximize the use of the time and expertise of the inclusion support teacher and other specialists providing support for the student with disabilities. It is especially helpful for teachers who think they may need support but are not sure what kinds of support are available to assist them in including a student with disabilities. Examples of both the Support Planning Grid and the Support Planning Menu for each of the students described in this section can be found following each student portrait.

Full Inclusion Support Planning Grid

Student: **Claire B.**

Age: **8**

Grade: **3**   General Education Teacher **Jacobo**

Class Schedule:

Inclusion Support Teacher **Ryan**

Date: **10/95**

School: **Miramonte**

Student's IEP Objectives	Opening	Language Arts	Recess	Math	Lunch	Science/ Soc. Stud.	Recess	Art/ Music	Dismiss			
Math: Identify coins & values				C, D / 5								
Follow 3rd gr. math curriculum				C, D / 5								
Quantity of work smaller-same time on task		C, D / 2,3		C, D		C, D / 2,3		C / 6				
Facilitate with at least 3 people	B / 5,6,or 8	B / 5,6 or 8		B / 5,8		B / 5,8		B / 5,8				
Stay in seat	E / 8	E / 5,8			A / 5 or 6							
Raise hand to request attention	E / 5	E / 5			A / 5 or 6	E / 6		E / 5				
Writing: Dictate to peer or adult		D / 3,5,8				C, D / 6,8		C, D / 8,9				
Check self after restroom			E / 5 or 8		E / 5 or 8		E / 5 or 8					
Speech: Improve sentence length		D / 2,3,or 5				E / 2,5		E / 5,6				
P.E.: Improve motor skills			A / 8				A / 8					

Key:

Curriculum Adaptations:
(A) As Is   (B) Physical Assistance   (C) Adapt Materials   (D) Multi-level Outcomes   (E) Goals Outside Content Area

Levels of Assistance:
(1) No Additional   (2) DIS/Related Service   (3) Inclusion Support Teacher   (4) Resource Teacher   (5) Aide   (6) Staff   (7) Cross Age Tutor   (8) Peers   (9) Parents

63

FULL INCLUSION SUPPORT PLANNING MENU

Student: *Claire*　　　　　　　　　　　　**Teacher:** *Mr. Jacobs*
Inclusion Support Teacher: *Ms. Williamson*　　**Activities for the month of:** *November*

Student Observation: *Observe at least once during langauge arts, math, and social studies/science to chart progress on wandering behavior goal.*	**Curriculum Adaptation:** *Check math worksheets for adaptations.* *Enlarge worksheets as needed.* *Check journal writing assignments for any necessary adaptations.* *Check teacher lesson plans for opportunities to meet other basic skill needs.*
Direct Work with Student: *Friday—Facilitate with computer during social studies unit.* *Work on use of restroom when aide is not available.*	**Instructional Strategies:** *At least once during each period of the day, monitor aides use of prompts.* *Schedule time to come to class to model appropriate behavior intervention (catch her being good).* *Make sure during her time in class, speech teacher models appropriate strategies to increase sentence length for aide and teacher.*
Assessment/Evaluation: *Check progress on IEP goals by reviewing worksheets and behavior checklists filled out by aide.*	**Classroom Activities:** *Teach at least two lessons from the science unit to the entire class to release teacher for prep time and to model above strategies for instructional assistant.* *Check-in with adaptive physical education teacher who teaches whole class each Tuesday/Thursday to see how things are going.*
Materials: *Enlarge worksheets and adapt journal assignments as needed.* *Complete behavior checklist for Claire's desk to help her chart her own progress.*	**Teacher Conference:** *Attend monthly meeting.* *Check-in during teacher's prep period each week.*
Parent Contact: *Call parent once a week.* *Leave message regarding classwork on answering machine for parent to check weekly.*	**Paperwork (IEP's, etc.):** *Make sure all signatures are on behavior support plan.*

A Day in the Life of Claire

Claire used to ride the small yellow bus to a special day class at a school about 40 minutes from her house. Now, Claire's mom drops her off on her way to work, and she is met by several friends who accompany her to class. The instructional assistant assigned to the classroom keeps an eye on Claire and her friends to make sure that they take the most direct route to the classroom, but she tries to stay out of the way. Upon arrival in class, Claire hangs up her backpack in the closet alongside her friends and goes to her desk. At the beginning of the year, the orientation and mobility specialist suggested that the path from the front door to the closet and then to Claire's desk be made as obstacle free as possible. Due to increased visual acuity, Claire is able to get around objects and to her desk without a problem. During the opening period, the instructional assistant reminds Claire to stay in her seat and prompts her to raise her hand when attendance is called.

During language arts, the general education teacher, instructional assistant, and peers who are sitting in Claire's group help her in a number of ways. Today, students are engaged in building a castle from sugar cubes, glue, and various art materials to coincide with the unit the class is doing on classic fairy tales. While Claire does not like getting her fingers sticky, she does enjoy listening to her peers read excerpts from the story. The teacher reminds Claire that before reading the story today, the students have to work on the design and building of the castle. So, the peers in Claire's group, along with Claire, decided that she would be responsible for distributing and collecting the materials and would provide suggestions regarding the design of the castle. It was OK with Claire and her peers if she did not want to get involved in the actual construction of the castle. Later during this period, the assistant helps Claire by writing a short entry for her journal on what life in a castle might have been like. Claire has contributed the words castle, scary, cold, and big.

Recess typically finds Claire at the swings, which is one of her favorite activities. There is no need for the instructional assistant to stay with Claire during this time as her peers usually look after her and play with her, and Claire responds well to the teacher on duty. At the beginning of the year, Claire's mother was worried that Claire did not have the strength or balance to swing safely. The occupational therapist assessed Claire, showed her where to grip the sides of the swings and how to scoot right onto the middle of the swing to maintain good balance. Since this initial consultation, Claire has fallen only once, and her peers often remind her to hang on tightly. A few minutes before recess is over, the instructional assistant joins

> During the opening period, the instructional assistant reminds Claire to stay in her seat and prompts her to raise her hand when attendance is called.

Claire and assists her in using the restroom. While she can take care of her toileting needs, she often forgets to check herself to make sure that her pants or skirt is buttoned properly. She sometimes will need help if the button is particularly difficult.

After recess, Claire and her peers are seated at their desks for math. Claire generally follows the third grade math curriculum with material modifications such as fewer problems per page and large print worksheets. The vision specialist has provided suggestions to the teacher and instructional assistant regarding the best ways to arrange the problems on the paper and how to highlight the space where she would put her answer. Her IEP also states that Claire will learn about the value of coins and independtly complete a money transaction by the end of the year. The site team decided that the best way to reinforce and teach these concepts would be to have Claire make purchases at a local store on a weekly basis. The inclusion support teacher is responsible for the development and implementation of this lesson. Once a week she meets with Claire and two nondisabled peers (all peers participate on a rotating basis throughout the year) to determine what they need at the store. Typically, they buy a snack for the class or food that the teacher may need for an upcoming activity. Important concepts for the lesson for Claire include identification of coin amounts needed for the transaction and independently giving the money to the cashier at the store. For her nondisabled peers the key concepts include adding and estimation.

At lunchtime Claire is seated with several peers and her instructional assistant. The assistant is needed to get Claire started as she typically has difficulty walking with her tray to the lunch table and opening the milk container. While her peers have offered assistance, the team decided that the beginning of lunch was an important instructional period for Claire. After the assistant has helped Claire to the table, she moves to the other side of the lunch area and allows Claire to interact with her peers. After she is finished eating, the instructional assistant is there again to help Claire gather her lunch tray and deposit it in the trash can. She and her peers then go to recess by themselves. The orientation and mobility instructor has shown Claire and her peers the best route to the playground and how to assist Claire to use the wall or a piece of equipment as support when there is a large crack in the sidewalk or when the texture of the ground changes (i.e., from concrete to the soft rubber pad under the equipment).

After lunch, the students in Claire's classroom are involved in sustained silent reading. During this twenty-minute period, Claire looks at a large print picture book and listens to a story on tape with head-

> While her peers have offered assistance, the team decided that the beginning of lunch was an important instructional period for Claire.

phones. Sometimes the instructional assistant or a peer reads quietly to her at her desk.

The afternoon curriculum includes social science and science on different days. The students have been working on a unit on maps and Claire has helped her group develop a map of their community. The speech and language specialist uses this activity as an opportunity to work on some of Claire's individualized communication needs. Claire is working on improving articulation, using new vocabulary words, and increasing her sentence length. Twice a week the specialist works with Claire and a small group of nondisabled peers who seem to need some additional support with vocabulary building. In today's activity the students are identifying key streets and landmarks around their school. This small group activity gives Claire the opportunity to use the words street, intersection, and crosswalk and to label the names of streets. The speech and language specialist models appropriate sentence lengths and prompts Claire to articulate appropriately.

The teacher lets Claire walk with her peers but keeps an eye on her until she is safely on the bus.

A short afternoon recess follows social science or science, and then the students have art and music on alternate days. As is true for many students, this period of the day is one of Claire's favorite (but only when it is music). She enjoys singing and using various musical instruments. No help is needed from her instructional assistant or peers, and this is one activity where no modifications to the curriculum are necessary. On the days when the class is having art, Claire is encouraged by the classroom teacher to use new art materials and to try new textures. She is reinforced for these attempts by being one of several students to distribute and collect art materials, which she enjoys doing.

At the end of the day, Claire lines up with the rest of her classmates and walks to the front of the school to wait for the after school day care van. Several of her classmates go with her, so she is not as hesitant to board the bus as she was at the beginning of the school year. The teacher lets Claire walk with her peers but keeps an eye on her until she is safely on the bus.

A Day in the Life of Tameka

It is a Monday morning, and the bell rings, signifying the start of the school day. Thirty fifth graders noisily begin to line up in front of Room 17 at the east end of campus. As the students find their places in line, designated by numbers, Tameka looks about for Jimmy and Nikki, the two students she must stand between in the morning line. By designating a specific order for all students in the morning line, the teacher is able to quickly see who is not yet present. This strategy also provides Tameka with the structure and consistency she needs to begin her day in an organized, predictable fashion. Once the students are lined up and quiet, the teacher welcomes the class and asks the students to greet each other. Each student says good morning or another greeting to the student in front of and behind him or her. This practice was originally started as part of classroom community building and has continued as a way for students to start the day with a welcoming interaction. This also helps Tameka work on her social skills, and she can also practice telling students that she needs more space in line instead of pushing or screaming as she had done previously.

The fifth graders in this class are a diverse group, and several students have special talents or needs. There are several students who are labeled as gifted and talented, some who are learning English as a second language, a few students with learning disabilities,and one student who is hearing impaired, along with Tameka who has a label of autism. The teacher prefers to use as many hands on and group activities for learning as possible to accommodate the range of abilities and needs with this particular group of students. These activities can mean that the noise level in the class gets high, and the structure can appear loose, both of which can cause Tameka to have difficulty managing her own behavior.

As the students enter the classroom, they turn in their homework packets and reading cards, put their coats and lunches in the closet, and get seated at their desk clusters. While the students are getting organized and settled at their desks, the instructional assistant who works with Tameka meets her at her desk cluster and reviews a picture schedule of the day's activities. The assistant will particularly emphasize and prepare Tameka for any unusual activities occurring that day such as a school assembly or classroom guest speaker. The more preparation Tameka can have for changes in routine, the more successful her day will be. Consequently, there are several strategies that Tameka is learning to be successful in this environment.

The picture on Tameka's schedule indicates that today's first activity will be journal writing. Around her, students are working on several different journal activities: shared writing with a friend, partner writing with an adult helper, and independent writing of stories, poems, illustrations, and thoughts about the day. Tameka gets her journal out of her desk and thumbs through a collection of magazine pictures that her mother has compiled in a notebook. Tameka chooses a picture of three children in a play and writes several lines in her journal, reciting the words as she writes them. The instructional

The more preparation Tameka can have for changes in routine, the more successful her day will be.

assistant records these sentences which Tameka re-copies on the next page of her journal. Because Tameka has difficulty with size and spacing, she copies her sentences on every other line and uses a finger space in between words.

During reader's workshop, students work in groups on activities related to the class novel, *Sounder* (Armstrong, 1989). Each group sets its own goals and schedule, choosing how many pages they will read on a given day. Each student in the group also has a particular job, and it is Tameka's responsibility to record the attendance of each group member. Once this is completed, the students begin reading. Although she is capable of reading this material on her own, Tameka usually takes turns reading aloud with a partner. This strategy helps her to remain focused and allows her to ask for clarification when she encounters an unfamiliar vocabulary word. When they are finished reading, the students will generate discussion questions for the group meeting. As she dictates her questions to a peer, it is easy to see how insightful Tameka is. She enjoys literature, and her questions often stimulate lively conversation. As she asks each question, Tameka works on maintaining eye contact and using an appropriate tone of voice. The speech and language specialist often provides consultation during this activity.

> Because Tameka has difficulty with size and spacing, she copies her sentences on every other line and uses a finger space in between words.

The writer's workshop activity for this day centers around the completion of pen pal letters that are being written to students in a curriculum methods course at a local university. On the previous day, Tameka had generated her ideas into a tape recorder. Her comments were then re-copied by the instructional assistant. Tameka is now typing the closing paragraph on the computer. When she is finished, she will decorate her letter and envelope. Tameka particularly likes this part of the pen pal project! Having just received new markers from her friend, Nikki, Tameka is excited to share her markers and trade stickers with her table partners.

During the word study activity, students are arranged in groups of six, playing concentration with this week's word study words. Tameka and her partner, Taryn, move to work on the carpet where the noise level is less distracting. As Tameka and Taryn match the word cards with the definitions, Tameka works on saying, "your turn" and "you got a match." The teacher monitors this group as she circulates among the other groups in the classroom.

The instructional assistant shows Tameka her schedule and reminds her that it is almost time for recess. Tameka takes an envelope out of her notebook and sorts through the picture cards in the envelope. Tameka selects a picture of play practice, and then she sorts through

69

a second set of pictures and chooses four friends: Johnny, Stephanie, Mark, and Gaela. She asks each child, "Do you want to be in my play?" Three students agree, but Stephanie has chosen to play four square instead. Tameka asks Julie next, and the new cast members walk out to an open area on the playground. For the next 15 minutes, Tameka provides dialogue and stage directions, and soon everyone is laughing. The instructional assistant reminds her when her words or tone are not friendly, and Tameka tries again. When the bell rings, the students walk to their designated places in line.

Today's math lesson begins with a review test on multiplication facts. On Tameka's test, the problems have been enlarged and separated, with each row outlined in a different color. After the students complete the test, they correct the test together. Anyone who graded a test with all of the answers right walks to the front of the classroom and announces, "I'm celebrating someone who got 100% on his/her math test." Tameka smiles as her name is called by her friend, Daniel.

> Once she has completed one of the word problems, Tameka hands the teacher a pink card, signaling that she needs to take a break.

During the second part of the math activity, the students break into groups where they are working on writing division word problems. The teacher has prepared a template so that Tameka only needs to fill in the missing words and numbers. Once she has completed one of the word problems, Tameka hands the teacher a pink card, signaling that she needs to take a break. Tameka leaves the room, walks once around the building, and then returns to her desk where she works on a division worksheet from her independent work folder.

The students have been studying colonial times in social studies and are presently practicing the skills and crafts prevalent in the early United States. Students are working at centers where they learn candle dipping, butter churning, bread making, and sampler sewing. Tameka chooses the bread making group, based on her interest in cooking. The parent volunteer helps her measure the ingredients, and Tameka quickly discovers that kneading bread is lots of fun. Once the bread is set aside to rise, Tameka and the other members of her group return to their seats to draw a picture and record their adventures in their colonial diaries.

When the bell rings for lunch, Tameka checks her schedule and then collects her lunch box and walks with her friends to the lunch area. Because she typically finishes her lunch quickly, Tameka has brought her markers and drawing paper along with her. Tameka, Daniel, and Julie take the art materials to the quiet play area where Tameka feels more comfortable than she does in the chaos on the playing field. Sometimes Tameka will choose to play on the bars with kids from other classes and show off her "skin the cat" expertise.

After recess, the students come back into the classroom for sustained silent reading time. Tameka, Evette, and Joey are sitting together, wearing headphones and listening to a tape of yesterday's literature discussion group. Once the timer has signaled the end of reading time, Carly shows Tameka the picture for science on her schedule and Tameka walks to her science group.

The students have been conducting science experiments and investigating the concept of variables. Today, they are working in scientific teams to predict and analyze the number and configuration of pennies necessary to sink a paper boat. Tameka is working with a group of three students, and she has chosen the job of counting and recording the numbers of pennies used in each trial. Tameka's partner, Verlain, has made a recording sheet for her, and he points out where to record the data. When the boat sinks, Tameka becomes uneasy and begins to shout. The teacher asks her to "use her words," and Tameka says finally that she does not like it when everyone pushes each other to rescue the sunken craft. It is agreed that the entire process will move more smoothly if the team members take turns removing the boat from the water, and the activity continues once again.

While the students copy the homework assignment from the board, Tameka copies her assignment from a card on her desk made by Jose, one of her classmates.

Once the science activities have been cleared away, Tameka returns to her desk and checks her schedule. "It's time to go home!" she announces. While the students copy the homework assignment from the board, Tameka copies her assignment from a card on her desk made by Jose, one of her classmates. She puts her homework assignment and her social studies book into her backpack and collects her lunch box. In order to be excused, each student must answer a review question from the day's activities. The teacher asks, "What is something in an experiment that can be changed?" and looks around the room. "Variable!" Tameka says loudly. The teacher reminds her to raise her hand, and Tameka tries again. This time she does it right, and the teacher taps Tameka on the shoulder to signal that she may leave the room.

Tameka puts her chair on her table and waves good-bye to Daniel, Nikki, and Julie. "Are you coming to my birthday party?" Julie calls. "Yes, I am!" Tameka shouts, smiling. This is her first birthday party invitation ever, and Tameka has been talking about the party all week. Then, with backpack and ponytail flying, Tameka runs across the playground to the van where her Mom is waiting.

Creating Caring Classrooms and School Communities

We believe that inclusion provides an opportunity for all children to share a learning environment full of rich experiences. The benefits of inclusion, however, go beyond accessing the core curriculum. Everyone benefits from being part of a community of learners where everyone belongs, everyone learns, and everyone receives the supports they need to do their personal best. By understanding, accepting, and celebrating human diversity within such communities of learners, children can feel a sense of belonging and learn to become vital members of a supportive and interdependent community of peers and adults. It is clear from both the research and from practice that inclusive educational practices can benefit all students in this manner and teachers, as well. But it is equally clear that the effectiveness and sustainability of inclusive education rests upon broader school reform and change. That is, inclusion of students with disabilities in general education classes will be most successful and sustainable when it is part of a broader effort to support all diverse learners within caring classrooms and school communities.

> We recognize that schools are at different places in regard to school reform and implementation of inclusive educational models.

We recognize that schools are at different places in regard to school reform and implementation of inclusive educational models. Some school communities are just beginning to think about how to best change their educational programs to meet the increasing diversity of students found in their classrooms today. Other schools have embraced reforms and have begun implementing comprehensive and longitudinal plans to better meet the diverse needs of students in their classrooms. This book provides information for parents, teachers, and others to use in developing and implementing successful inclusion opportunities. This information on the more technical aspects of implementing an inclusive model for education provides the solid foundation upon which all children's academic growth and emotional well being can be built. As school reform advocates work for system-wide change, individual teachers, parents, and others have the ability to make immediate and significant changes in the lives of individual children currently within those educational systems. We hope that this book provides the impetus and the information to facilitate such important change.

References

Armstrong, T. (1994). Multiple intelligences in the classroom. Alexandria, VA: Association for Supervision and Curriculum Development.

Armstrong, W. (1989). Sounder. New York: Harper & Row.

Bishop, K. D., & Jubala, K. A. (1995). Positive Behavior Support Strategies. In M. Falvey (Ed.), Inclusive and heterogeneous schooling: Assessment, curriculum, and instruction (pp. 159–186). Baltimore: Paul H. Brookes.

Carbo, M. (1995). Educating everybody's children. In R. W. Cole (Ed.), Educating everybody's children: Diverse teaching strategies for diverse learners (pp. 1–7). Alexandria, VA: Association for Supervision and Curriculum Development.

Carle, E. (1987). The very hungry caterpillar. New York: Philomel Books.

Carr, E. G., Robinson, S., & Palumbo, L. W. (1990). The wrong issue: Aversive vs. nonaversive treatment. The right issue: Functional vs. nonfunctional treatment. In A. Repp & N. Singh (Eds.), Perspectives on the use of nonaversive and aversive interventions for persons with developmental disabilities. Sycamore, IL: Sycamore Publishing Co.

Coots, J. J., Bishop, K. D., Grenot-Scheyer, M., & Falvey, M. (1995). Practices in general education: Past and present. In, M. Falvey (Ed.), Inclusive and heterogeneous schooling: Assessment, curriculum, and instruction (pp.7–22). Baltimore: Paul H. Brookes

Dewey, J. (1956). The child and the curriculum: The school and society. Chicago: University of Chicago Press.

Dinkmeyer, D., McKay,G., & Dinkmeyer, D., Jr. (1980). Systematic training for effective teaching. Circle Pines: American Guidance Service.

Falvey, M., Grenot-Scheyer, M., Coots, J. J., & Bishop, K. D. (1995). Services for students with disabilities: Past and present. In M. Falvey (Ed.), Inclusive and heterogeneous schooling: Assessment, curriculum, and instruction (pp. 23–39). Baltimore: Paul H. Brookes.

Forest, M., & Lusthaus, E. (1989). Promoting educational equality for all students: Circles and maps. In S. Stainback, W. Stainback, & M. Forest (Eds.), Educating all students in the mainstream of regular education (pp. 43–57). Baltimore: Paul H. Brookes.

Gardner, H. (1983). Multiple intelligences: The theory in practice. New York: Basic Books.

Giangreco, M. F., Dennis, R., Cloninger, C., Edelman, S., & Shattman, R. (1993). "I've counted Jon": Transformational experiences of teachers educating students with disabilities. Exceptional Children, 59(4), 359–372.

Gibbs, J. (1995). TRIBES: A new way of learning and being together. Sausalito, CA: Center Source Systems.

Hunt, P., Staub, D., Alwell, M., & Goetz, L. (1994). Achievement by all students within the context of cooperative learning groups. The Journal of The Association for Persons with Severe Handicaps, 19(4), 290–301.

Jenkins, J. R., Jewell, M., O'Connor, R. E., Jenkins, L. M., & Troutner, N. M. (1994). Accomodations for individual differences without classroom ability groups: An experiment in school restructuring. Exceptional Children, 60(4), 344–358.

Johnson, D. W. & Johnson, R. T. (1989). Cooperation and competition: Theory and research. Edina, MN: Interaction Books.

Jubala, K. A., Bishop, K. D., & Falvey, M. (1995). Creating a supportive classroom environment. In M. Falvey (Ed.), Inclusive and heterogeneous schooling: Assessment, curriculum, and instruction (pp.111–129). Baltimore: Paul H. Brookes.

Levine, D., Lowe, R., Peterson, B., & Tenorio, R. (1995). Rethinking schools: An agenda for change. New York: The New Press.

Meyer, L. H. (1994). Understanding the impact of inclusion (special issue). The Journal of the Association for Persons with Severe Handicaps, 19(4), 251-332.

National Coalition of Advocates for Students (1991). The good common school: Making the vision work for all children. Boston: National Coalition of Advocates for Students.

Neary, T. & Mintun, B. (1991). Classroom activity analysis worksheet. Sacramento: California State Department of Education.

O'Neil, J. (1994–1995). Can inclusion work? A conversation with Jim Kauffman and Mara Sapon-Shevin. Educational Leadership, 52(4), 7–11.

Staub, D., & Peck, C. A. (1994-1995). What are the outcomes for nondisabled students? Educational Leadership, 52(4), 36–40.

Tharp, R. G., & Gallimore, R. (1988). Rousing minds to life: Teaching, learning, and schooling in social context. New York: Cambridge University Press.

Thousand, J., & Villa, R. (1990). Sharing expertise and responsibilities through teaching teams. In W. Stainback & S. Stainback (Eds.), Support networks for inclusive schooling: Interdependent integrated education (pp. 201-218). Baltimore: Paul H. Brookes.

Udvari-Solner, A. (1994). A decision-making model for curricular adaptations in cooperative groups. In J. Thousand, R. Villa, & A. Nevin (Eds.), Creativity and collaborative learning (pp.59-77). Baltimore: Paul H. Brookes.

Udvari-Solner, A. (1992). Accomodating the instructional needs of diverse learners in the context of general education. Topeka, KS: Kansas State Board of Education (ERIC Report No. ED354685).

Preparation of this book was supported in part by Cooperation Agreement No. H086A20003 to Syracuse University, with a sub-contract to California State University, Long Beach from the Office of Special Education Programs, U.S. Department of Education. This material does not necessarily reflect the position or policies of the U.S. Department of Education, and no official endorsement should be inferred.

Teacher Created Materials
Resource List

TCM 059 Learning Centers Through the Year

TCM 147 Activities for Any Literature Unit

TCM 244 Plants—Thematic Unit

TCM 353 Literature Activities for Reluctant Readers (Primary)

TCM 354 Literature Activities for Reluctant Readers (Intermediate)

TCM 482 Values in Literature

TCM 504 Portfolios and Other Assessments

TCM 508 Celebrate Our Similarities

TCM 601 Celebrating Diversity—Extended Theme

TCM 605 Heroes Interdisciplinary Unit

TCM 620 Courage Interdisciplinary Unit

TCM 650 Cooperative Learning Activities for Language Arts (Primary)

TCM 652 Cooperative Learning Activities for Social Studies (Challenging)

TCM 665 Using Multicultural Literature: Overcoming Difficulties

TCM 890 Motivating At-Risk Students